50
ways

to succeed as an
international student

Stella Cottrell

 macmillan
international
HIGHER EDUCATION

 RED GLOBE
PRESS

First published 2019 by
RED GLOBE PRESS

Red Globe Press in the UK is an imprint of Springer Nature Limited, registered in England, company number 785998, of 4 Crinan Street, London, N1 9XW.

Red Globe Press® is a registered trademark in the United States, the United Kingdom, Europe and other countries.

ISBN 978–1–352–00576–9 paperback

This book is printed on paper suitable for recycling and made from fully managed and sustained forest sources. Logging, pulping and manufacturing processes are expected to conform to the environmental regulations of the country of origin.

A catalogue record for this book is available from the British Library.

A catalog record for this book is available from the Library of Congress.

Contents

50 Ways

Acknowledgements

I would like to acknowledge my warmest thanks to those involved in the production of this book, especially Georgia Park and Amy Brownbridge for producing books within the series; Jayne Martin-Kaye for text design; Barbara Wilson for copyediting; Genevieve Friar for proofreading; and Helen Caunce for her oversight and support. I am especially grateful to Claire Dorer and Georgia Park for the innumerable tasks they have undertaken to enable the production of the series, their care over the details and their generous encouragement and goodwill.

"Globe" icon by Ralf Schmitzer, p. x; "House" icon by Numero Uno, p. xxi; "Exam" icon by Nociconist, p. xxi; "Tickets" icon by Ricardo Martins, p. xxi; "Writing" icon by Laurin Kraan, p. xxi; "Help" icon by Gregor Cresnar, p. xxii; "Laptop" icon by B. Agustín Amenábar Larraín, p. xxii; "Ship" icon by Jenya K, p. 2; "Sushi" icon by Made by Made, p. 7; "Paris" icon by CJS, p. 7; "Taj Mahal" icon by Lastspark, p. 7; "Balloon" icon by Walle_Chan, p. 7; "Finish" icon by Adrien Coquet, p. 9; "Aim" icon by Setyo Ari Wibowo, p. 10; "Visa" icon by Nakul Dhaka, p. 14; "Route" icon by BomSymbols, p. 15; "Airport" icon by Tokyo Monorail, p. 16; "Money" icon by Adrien Coquet, p. 22; "Piggy bank" icon by Numero Uno, p. 23; "Conversation" icon by Shashank Singh, p. 27; "Stage" icon by Juan Pablo Bravo, p. 29; "University" icon by Pham Duy Phuong Hung, p. 29; "House" icon by Symbolon, p. 31; "Potted plant" icon by Alex Muravev, p. 31; "Network" icon by Matt Hawdon, p. 33; "Flag" icon by Alfa Design, p. 34; "TV" icon by Creative Stall, p. 39; "World" icon by Anton Barbarov, p. 40; "Language" icon by Nociconist, p. 41; "Conversation" icon by Viktor Ostrovsky, p. 43; "Pizza slice" icon by Vectors Market, pp. 43, 105; "Group discussion" icon by Shastry, p. 43; "Coffee" icon by James, p. 43; "Family" icon by Gan Khoon Lay, p. 43; "Musical note" icon by Mikicon, p. 43; "Swot analysis" icon by Bold Yellow, p. 49; "Coordinated assessment" icon by OCHA Visual, p. 49; "Helpfulness" icon by Yu Luck, p. 53; "Audio book" icon by Artworkbean, p. 55; "Movie" icon by Rose Alice Design, p. 55; "Owl" icon by Maxim Kulikov, p. 59; "Person" icon by Hat-Tech, p. 63; "Conversation" icon by Adrien Coquet, p. 65; "Sport" icon by Pause08, p. 66; "Sport" icon by Tomas Knopp, p. 67; "Laughing emoji" icon by Mooms, p. 69; "Books" icon by Jakub Čaja, p. 73; "Lecture room" icon by Llisole, p. 72; "Running watch" icon by Charlotte Vogel, p. 75; "Science report" icon by Llisole, p. 77;

"Grade" icon by Bieu Tuong, p. 77; "Blog" icon by Dilakuscan, p. 79; "Bubble bath" icon by HeadsOfBirds, p. 81; "Yoga" icon by Mariia Nisiforova, p. 81; "Water" icon by Naveen, p. 81; "Exam" icon by Gregor Cresnar, p. 85; "Vote" icon by Adrien Coquet, p. 93; "Group discussion" icon by Aneeque Ahmed, p. 95; "Group" icon by Rose Alice Design, p. 99; "Shooting star" icon by Focus Lab, p. 101; "Library" icon by Rich Paul, p. 103; "Chicken" icon by Anbileru Adaleru, p. 105; "Croissant" icon by AomAm, p. 105; "Pineapple" icon by Creaticca Creative Agency, p. 105; "Cake" icon by Francielly Costantin Senra, p. 105; all from the Noun Project (www.thenounproject.com).

About this book

This book suggests 50 Ways towards success as an international student. It covers many aspects of life and study, including:

- Ways to prepare before travelling for your course

- Ways to settle in and cope with life and study in a new country

- Ways to achieve academic success

- Ways to gain the most from the experience, so you learn and develop as a person and enjoy yourself too.

Many of the Ways involve socialising and well-being, so can be fun as well as useful!

Just a taste ...
This is a small book with many big ideas. Each 'Way' is a starting point, offering suggestions of things to do and to think about. Browse these to spark ideas of your own. You may find this initial taste is enough in itself to spur you to action – or you can follow up suggestions using the resources recommended.

Map your own route
Each student is different, so the best combination of actions will be unique to you. Start with page ix, and then select freely from the 50 Ways to suit your own needs and interests. Be open and adventurous in your approach: try out things you might not usually consider.

The 50 Ways series
This series is especially useful for international students, including those studying in English as an 'additional' or 'foreign' language.

How to use this book

Get started
Begin with the introduction
and Ways 1–5.

Discover
Find out about things you can do to have a happier
and more successful time as an international student.

Become more self-aware
Find out more about yourself through
trying out different things.

Reflect
Use the mini self-evaluations to focus your thinking. Then
consider possible ways forward suggested by your answers.

Choose
Decide which of the 50 Ways you want to
try out. You don't have to do them all!

Commit
Once you decide to commit to something, put your
whole self behind your decision. Do it!

Shape new habits
As you learn, form new habits that support your
success for the longer term. See page x.

Find out more
Follow up using the recommended resources if you wish.
See pages 114–17 or use the reference list to follow up
sources numbered in superscript in the text.

Shape new habits and ways of thinking

Living and studying in a new country usually involves changing the way you approach your study and everyday living. Making such changes, although unsettling at times, can enrich your life, boost your employability and help you to thrive in an increasingly international world. Whilst there is so much change in your life, it is a great time to reconsider how you do things – and why. You can start to form new habits that could benefit you for life.

Use 50 Ways ... for habit-building

Act

Be active in shaping new habits and ways of thinking. Most pages of this book provide opportunities to reflect, choose, decide and commit.

Commit

Place yourself fully behind your good intentions by using the 'I will' boxes. Be selective: you don't need to commit to all of the 50 Ways. Decide which are the most important actions for investing your time and energies.

Track

Keep track of your good intentions. It usually takes at least 6–8 weeks to form new habits. If you wish, you can use:

- pages 108–9 to track and monitor new habits you want to form

- pages 110–11 to track your progress with any of the Ways you try out

- pages 112–13 for your 20+ things to do whilst an international student.

The international student community

A growing trend

As an international student, you are part of a growing worldwide community of people who have taken the adventurous decision to study in a new country.[1,2] There has been an 'explosion' in numbers studying abroad, from 800,000 in the 1970s to 4.6 million by 2015.[3,4]

An important part of the student community

Around 10% of postgraduates and 5% of undergraduates, globally, are international students. The USA, UK and China are the most popular destinations.[5,6] Undergraduate intakes are low in some countries and more heavily international in others,[3] although this varies by institution so check figures for those that interest you. Countries with high proportions of international undergraduates include Luxembourg (25%), Austria (18%), New Zealand (16%), UK (14%) and Australia (13%).

Who goes where?

International students come from all around the world. Around 20%, globally, are from China, 7% India, 4% Germany, and 2–3% each from Korea, France and Saudi Arabia. Most study in English-speaking countries or where English is the medium of instruction.

The pattern of international intakes varies by country. Chinese students study mainly in the USA, UK and Australia. China attracts students from Indonesia and Korea. Almost a quarter of international students are European and study in another European country. In Russia, two-thirds are from countries with historical links to the former Soviet Union. In France, 41% of international students are from Africa.[3]

International study: A fantastic opportunity

Exercise choice

As an international student, you get to choose from a much wider range of courses and qualifications worldwide, in dozens of countries. There are options for being abroad for just a few weeks or months or 1–2 years as well as for the whole qualification. Choose what suits your circumstances, interests and personality best. See page 114 for sites that help in selecting courses.

Enjoy new experiences

International study isn't just a way of gaining a qualification; it provides a wonderful way of gaining a huge range of new experiences. Some you can plan, but there will be lots of surprises too!

Open up your world

As an international student, you get to travel, see a new country, meet a wide range of people and experience what it is really like to live in a culture different to your own. The country of study might also be a stepping stone to visiting other nearby countries, too.

Be part of a global international community

Taking that step to travel in order to study enters you into a new community of students worldwide who share similar sets of attitudes and experiences. Whether on campus or through social media, that creates fantastic opportunities to bond with people you might never have met otherwise, and to create exciting networks that might benefit your future.

Improve language skills

If you want to learn or perfect your proficiency in a foreign language, then studying abroad creates an ideal way to do this. Even if you are studying in your first language, you can discover interesting differences in the way that the language is used elsewhere.

New benefits, new challenges
Research shows that international study brings a unique set of experiences, both beneficial and challenging. Consider the main benefits and challenges for you. (See Ways 1 and 2.)

Develop as a person
Travelling, studying or working overseas means discovering new methods of doing things, including learning to cope with the unexpected and finding ways of resolving a wide range of potential obstacles. This tends to lead to greater maturity as well as a broader range of knowledge, skills and personal insights.

Realise new potential
It is likely that living and studying internationally will stretch you. You could uncover aspects of yourself you didn't expect, and find that you are capable of much more than you knew. Greater self-awareness is an asset. The more you do, the more you know about your limits and potential.

Boost your confidence
Surviving and thriving in a different country can strengthen you, increasing your confidence for coping in new situations and unexpected circumstances. You become more aware of how much you can change and adapt – and still be you.

Prepare ahead to manage the challenges

The challenges of international study are an integral part of the learning experience.[7,8,9,10] They provide opportunities to understand the world, learn new things, develop problem-solving skills and gain coping mechanisms. All these can become advantages that help you to succeed better in life.

What kinds of challenges?

Cultural differences: There are likely to be many aspects of the culture of the host country that surprise and possibly even shock you.[11] Whilst this can delight, it can mean rethinking the way you do things.[12,13] See Ways 13, 15 and 18.

Social integration: It can take repeated effort to meet people, make friends and feel you belong. Many universities now provide schemes to help social integration.[14] See Ways 11, 14 and 18.

Finances: Money matters pre-occupy many students, both home and international. It is essential to investigate the full costs of life and study and make financial arrangements to cover all of these. Don't assume you will find a part-time job to pay your way. Before making a commitment, check visa requirements, the availability of jobs, hours you would need to work and likely salary. See Ways 7 and 10.

Developing career opportunities: Whilst study abroad can strengthen career prospects long-term, this isn't always the case. Check whether the qualification you gain will be recognised in the country where you intend to work. Also, if you want career-related work whilst a student, find out what will be available so that your expectations are realistic. See Ways 40, 42 and 43.

Language and study skills: Teaching methods and academic conventions vary from one country to another.[15] (See page xv.) It is important to find out what these are, become used to them and adapt your approach. Studying in a foreign language offers a unique way of seeing how different languages shape the way we express ideas. You gain a sense of the subtle distinctions that can then arise from one language, or culture, to the next. See Ways 20, 22, 23 and 25.

Independent living: The everyday basics of cooking, shopping, laundry, travelling, organising and planning can seem complicated at first. A student experience survey in 2017 found a third of non-EU international students and a fifth of UK/EU students found this stressful.[16] Sharing tips is a good way to make new friends, develop autonomy and gain confidence.

Completing – or leaving early: Whilst most international students do stay to the end of the course and are successful in gaining their qualifications, a relatively high proportion leave early. Being committed to completing your course is an important task to consider. See Way 4.

Bring the right attitude

It is useful to nurture a positive attitude – and to interpret difficulties as temporary hurdles or puzzles that stretch your imagination to find solutions. On difficult days, you may not always feel like creative problem-solving, but it can be a gift to yourself to take home. See Way 6.

Remember you don't need to struggle on alone!

Finding ways of resolving challenges can be fun but can be stressful too. You don't have to do everything on your own. Use the available support services either in your host country or back home. Share experiences and problem-solving with other students. See page xxiii.

Different countries. Different ways to study

Teaching and assessment methods vary between countries – although changes you experience might arise from studying at a higher level, taking new subjects or teacher preferences rather than national differences. Below are key aspects to investigate, ideally before starting your course. Give yourself time to become used to any differences.

Differences to watch out for

Teaching and learning: the amount of face-to-face time with teaching staff; the proportion of time spent in class; the amount of groupwork and autonomous learning; whether class-time involves mainly listening and taking notes, or more active participation such as question and answer sessions, quizzes, discussion and student presentations.

Classroom behaviours: whether students listen without interrupting or ask questions; how you address teachers and peers; the level of formality and politeness; whether you can check messages or use phones during class; how closely you need to pay attention; the level of active participation expected.[17,18,19]

Structure: whether the course has a detailed syllabus or is loosely structured so you shape your own learning; whether study time is strongly organised for you or whether you manage time yourself.[20]

Assessment: the proportion of assessment using exams, coursework, multiple choice, written papers, groupwork, presentations or other assessments; how frequently you are tested and the weight given to each assessment; variations in the kind of answers that attract good grades, especially for written work. (See Way 38.)

Use of language: even if the course is taught in your home language, there can be unexpected differences. If studying in a foreign language, study tasks can take much longer; it might feel as though you are studying for two degrees, your main subject and the host language.

Reading: how much reading you have to do; whether there is a core textbook, a recommended list, or just suggestions to help you start your own searches of what to read.

Research and treatment of source material: whether you collect research data for yourself; whether you should critique sources; the kind of critique expected; how you use and refer to expert sources in your own writing; rules and penalties related to plagiarism and cheating.

Critical thinking/respect for experts: whether the emphasis is on critiquing what you hear, see and read and exploring ideas yourself OR on demonstrating close attention to details presented by tutors.[18,20]

Reflection about learning: whether this forms part of the course and its assessment; whether you need to keep a journal or log of the process by which you arrived at creative ideas, problem-solving, professional insights or understandings about your learning.[21]

Feedback: the amount you receive; whether feedback is written or verbal, individual or group, face to face or electronic, continually during everyday interactions with tutors or only once work is completed, etc.

Clarity or ambiguity: some cultures prize clarity and precision; others consider it important to leave 'grey areas' for people to make their own inferences and interpretations.[21]

Social time: differences in the relative emphasis on study, sports, pets, socialising, partying, food, photographs, family, culture, etc.[12,22]

Manage the 'culture shock'

It is not unusual to experience a certain amount of disorientation when you move to a new place – referred to as 'culture shock'. Sometimes this is because so much is new; other times it is because you just weren't expecting things to be quite so different.

Culture shock can be experienced as a process with several stages (see opposite). Knowing about these can help you to make sense of your experience. You might find that you go through these once, or as a cycle at the start of new term or module of study, or if you move campus, or after long visits home.

Getting through it

Understand
Recognise which stage you are in now.

Be kind to yourself
Be patient with your moods. Acknowledge the feelings. Plan things to enjoy or distract you in the meantime.

Pep talk
Remind yourself that the worst stages are finite – they won't last forever.

Don't rush home
Give yourself time to become familiar with your new situation – by being in it!

De-stress
Take steps to manage undue stress and restore a sense of calm.

Re-discover
Give yourself the chance to find out what there is to enjoy in the experience.

Stage 1 Honeymoon

Everything is exciting, intriguing, stimulating, and you are looking forward to the experience. You are open to discovery and trying out new things. You may feel euphoria, and be delighted by the differences with home. You still feel the connection with home.

Stage 2 Disenchantment

The novelty wears off, you miss familiar things and feel exhausted, irritated, homesick or overwhelmed by the changes. You focus mainly on what you find lacking, confusing, tiring or annoying.

Stage 3 Rejection

You feel hostile to people and things around you, idealise things back home and might wish you hadn't decided to study abroad. You reject much of what the opportunity has to offer.

Stage 4 Acclimatisation

You start to get used to your surroundings and accept differences more easily. The life becomes more familiar: you know what to expect and how things work. You have more energy and make more effort to join in and enjoy yourself.

Stage 5 Harmony

You feel very at home in the new country or culture. You know how things work and have your own routine and acquaintances. You are able to enjoy yourself and have a realistic appreciation of both home and the host country.

What international students say ...

Articles and blogs written by students are great for finding out about the day by day experience of being an international student.

Cultural difference
It is hard to predict what might surprise you. International students have reported being shocked at such differences as people wearing or not wearing shoes indoors or putting shoes on furniture; making or not making eye contact; how noisy or quiet students from some countries seem; or that strangers gave them friendly greetings.[11,23]

Similarities and differences
Even when the language and education system are apparently similar to home, there can be significant changes to manage. One student found there was more emphasis on weekly tests, class participation and group work for her Australian rather than her UK course. She had to rethink her approach to study, assessment and working with others.[13] Conversely, even where cultures differ, you can find similarities with home and with students from other countries.[24]

Attitudes towards 'time'
International students comment on differences in attitudes towards time. Attitudes are very relaxed in some countries, but others emphasise punctuality, filling time with activity, tight deadlines and penalties for lateness. This can affect any aspect of your day, such as fitting in with when others eat, sleep, socialise or meet for group projects. You might need to adapt your approach to time and time management.[12,13,24]

Enjoyment and value
Students write enthusiastically about study abroad.[18,23,25,26] Even students who describe challenges in adapting to studying abroad speak highly about the experience.[12,13]

Read student articles about their experiences!

Gain a sense of how other students coped with diverse aspects of international life and study, what they discovered, where they struggled and what they loved about it. For full details, see pages 118–24.

Accommodation

- USA student living with family in UK[27]

- UK student on halls and shared houses in Australia.[13]

Differences in teaching, assessment and grading

- USA compared to the UK[27]

- Japan compared to the UK[21]

- UK compared to Australia[13]

- Saudi Arabia compared to the UK[19]

- Western methods compared to Hong Kong.[18]

Social integration and student life

- Students from four continents[24]

- Chinese students in the USA[17]

- Russian student in Scotland[28]

- Spanish student in UK.[12]

Writing in a different language

- Writing essays: (East European in UK).[29]

International Student Blogs

Student blogs are great for putting your own experiences into perspective and picking up useful tips. Here are a few to get you started.

Africa: Aderotoye, O. (2017) Studying in Ghana: The Best Decision I've Ever Made, www.isepstudyabroad.org/articles/474

Australia: Khadim, M. (2017) Life As An International Student in Australia; MadihaKhadim Blogs.PinoyAu.info

Australia: www.timeshighereducation.com/student/blogs/international-perspective-zambian-student-australia

China: Thestudyabroadblog.com – Daily life as an international student in China

China: www.isepstudyabroad.org – Student stories of studying in China

India: Studyingabroad.co.in – Indian students in USA, UK, Canada and France

Japan: www.studyjapan.go.jp/en/faq/faq02e.html

UK: (London) Matsumoto[25,26]

USA: Studyusa.com – Life as an international student in the USA

Varied countries: internationalstudent.com; www.timeshighereducation.com/student/blogs

Using advice and support services

Finding help and support

Traditionally, international students have under-used available services such as counselling, medical services, study, library, health, mental health and peer mentoring.[30,31,32,33,34] When they do use services such as peer mentoring, they gain multiple benefits. (See Way 46.)

Whatever services are provided are there for you to use. It is likely that support staff will be familiar with enquiries about everything from loneliness, homesickness, study, money, medical enquiries, language classes, to disabilities and severe health conditions. You shouldn't ever feel that you can't ask for help.

If you are from a country or culture where students are wary of asking for help, do not miss out on help that other students are gaining. Enquiries are normally confidential but you can ask about this at your first contact.

Be prepared for support services to differ in each country, as they will possibly be much more diverse, or restricted, than you are used to.

When to seek support

- If you need information
- To understand the academic expectations and requirements
- If you don't understand 'how things work here'
- If you need language support or help in understanding the culture

- If you feel unsafe
- If you feel homesick, isolated, lonely, stressed or anxious
- If you are struggling to cope or neglecting things such as eating socialising, getting to class
- If you abuse drugs or alcohol, or self-harm or think about suicide.

Don't wait for an emergency: find out early on what is available and how to access support if needed.

1

Focus on the benefits

Anchor your positivity

 Do I ...?

1. Do I have a clear sense of the benefits to me of international study?

Yes ☐ No ☐

2. Do I have a list of these to motivate me at difficult times?

Yes ☐ No ☐

3. Am I aware of the skills and qualities I could develop?

Yes ☐ No ☐

4. Am I making the most of the experience?

Yes ☐ No ☐

Why is this important?

International study is exciting. It opens up great opportunities and can be a fantastic experience.[12] It is likely that you will gain skills, qualities and maturity that you wouldn't do otherwise. However, it isn't an easy option. At times, it can be hard and stressful. At such moments, it is helpful if you already have a strong appreciation of its benefits for you, now and longer term. Clarify these to yourself at a time when you are feeling good about your decision.[13] Keep adding to your list.

Considering your responses

If you hadn't really thought about the benefits or made a list to inspire yourself, start by using the list opposite. Add other items that are important to you. You could convert these into a bright chart to inspire you at the start of each day – or on days that feel more of a struggle.

 To do. I will ...

 See also Ways 2, 15, 23, 42

Identify the benefits to you

Below are some benefits of international study. Circle those of value to you. Then jot down any others that matter to you.

A good qualification	Seeing the world	**Write any other things here ...**
Academic skills	Stretching my mind	
Learning the language	Gaining new insights	
Other new skills	Sharpening my critical awareness	
Experiencing a new culture	Greater empathy	
Greater inter-cultural awareness	Improving career and employment choices	
Making friends internationally	Opening up new work or study opportunities	
Developing ability to communicate with a wider range of people	Personal challenge	
Networks/contacts	Greater maturity	

2 Recognise potential challenges

Tackle these and get stronger

Why is this important?

If you are aware of the things that could be difficult or that might go wrong, then you are in a better place to prevent or manage these. Thinking about these early makes it more likely that you will find a solution or the right help. Even if you can't avoid all problems, it is easier to cope if these do not come as unexpected surprises. Managing challenges provides you with new skills and insights. It builds your confidence and demonstrates that you can survive difficult situations and solve problems.

Considering your responses

If everything is going well, that is great! It is still useful to identify and plan for challenges that could lie ahead. If student life feels difficult now, clarify the issues so you can decide a plan of action. It can help to know that challenges such as those opposite are not unusual, and students do devise ways to cope and succeed. It is likely you can too!

 See also Ways 3, 4, 5, 6

? Do I ...?

1. Do I have a realistic sense of the challenges?

   Yes ☐ No ☐

2. Do I know the difficulties to anticipate?

   Yes ☐ No ☐

3. Do I feel proud to be tackling challenges like these that will strengthen me?

   Yes ☐ No ☐

 To do. I will ...

Identify challenges relevant to you

Below are some ways that international study can be especially challenging.
Select ✔ those most relevant to you.

- [ ] **Not knowing what to expect.**
- [ ] **Studying in a foreign language.**
- [ ] **Teaching methods are different to those at home.**
- [ ] **Tutors expect different things from me than at home.**
- [ ] **Homesickness.**
- [ ] **Loneliness/difficulty meeting new people.**
- [ ] **I don't understand what other people are saying.**
- [ ] **Feeling that I don't 'fit in'.**
- [ ] **Money/financial difficulties.**
- [ ] **Hard to find food I like.**
- [ ] **I don't feel confident about speaking in class.**
- [ ] **Nothing is the same.**
- [ ] **It is tiring.**
- [ ] **Don't know where to find help.**

Other things? Jot them down

3 Be prepared for the unexpected

Welcome opportunity – try out a whole new world!

Why is this important?

It is likely you will find many things are different from what you are used to at home.[11] Some will be pleasant surprises; others could be strange, disappointing or difficult. Humans are creatures of habit, so if you start to feel overwhelmed by the unfamiliar, it is tempting to retreat to a safe place and seek out people and things you know. That can be comforting – but strike a balance. Keep yourself happy, safe and secure, but also expect things to be different. 'Go with the flow' rather than finding ways to resist change. Enjoy the novelty in your new experience whilst you have this chance.[12]

Considering your responses

Consider whether your responses indicate that you are making every effort to find out what is available to you and to find interest and enjoyment in time abroad. If you say 'no' to many things that are different, consider saying 'yes' more often. You could discover much to enjoy. Don't wait for opportunities – make them!

 See also Ways 5, 11, 14, 26, 37

? Do I ...?

1. Do I encourage myself to get as much as possible out of this experience?

   Yes ☐ No ☐

2. Do I research things to do?

   Yes ☐ No ☐

3. Do I try out lots of new things?

   Yes ☐ No ☐

4. Do I create opportunities for myself?

   Yes ☐ No ☐

 To do. I will ...

Enjoy the adventure!

Research opportunities open to you

Use sites for tourists and international students, as well as your uni. Monitor sites frequently and talk to other students – don't miss out.

Travel widely

… in the region, the country and local countries.

Have a go!

Use every opportunity to take part in activities, eat new foods or see sights that might never come round again!

Plan for variety

Look for a wide range of things to do, to make the experience richer. Add these to your list of 20+ (pages 112–13).

Create opportunities

Don't stick to the same people all the time. Spend time in social spaces. Find things to do and to join. Start your own society or club, large or small. Organise things for yourself and others to do.

4

Commit to finishing the course

Promise yourself success

(?) Do I ...?

1. Do I have a strong commitment to finishing my course?
   Yes ☐ **No** ☐

2. Do I have clear aims?
   Yes ☐ **No** ☐

3. Do I take the right actions for completing this course to the end?
   Yes ☐ **No** ☐

4. Do I want to do this – for me?
   Yes ☐ **No** ☐

Why is this important?

Finishing your course reflects well on you. It shows other people and future employers that you can take on such a challenge and complete it. You also gain more from the experience. It is wise to be aware that, whilst most international students complete the course, a high proportion do not.[35] Your first step is to make a mental commitment to complete it. That is your decision. Be determined to do what it takes to finish. The reward is your qualification but also the knowledge and satisfaction that you succeeded – an accomplishment to carry with you through life.

Considering your responses

Consider whether your responses suggest that you are fully committed to your course and that you are doing this because you want to. If you are, then great. If not, make a decision to be one of those students who succeed in finishing what they set out to do. Make the experience count.

 To do. I will ...

 See also Ways 2, 5, 12, 42

Be there at the finishing line!

Indicate ✔ when you have completed each stage below.

Decide how much it matters
Consider why it matters to you to finish. Write that down.

Make it personal
Don't do it just to please someone else. Find your own reasons for finishing the course. Make completing it a source of personal pride.

Make a commitment
Make a mental commitment. Tell yourself that you are going to finish. Decide you will do what is necessary to get to the end.

Put it in writing
Put yourself behind your decision and remember why you made it: write down your commitment and your reasons. Keep this where you will see it – for inspiration!

Devise a strategy
Making the commitment is the first step. You now need to think how to make that a reality – your strategy for making it happen. See Way 5.

5 Devise a strategic plan

Plan your route to success

Why is this important?

You have already invested time and effort to get this far in your international adventure. There is much to be gained now, but it is wise to anticipate potential obstacles and setbacks. If you want to be one of the success stories, it is prudent to devise a strategy. Let this cover your aims, what you want to do and achieve, and actions you need to take to achieve these. Consider potential problems, solutions and sources of help. Having a plan puts you more in control of the outcomes. You might need to adapt it later but it is good to start with a plan.

Considering your responses

If your responses suggest that you don't have a clear plan, don't panic! It is worth thinking about the different elements of the plan opposite. What do each of these mean for you and your circumstances? Then devise your plan.

 See also Ways 2, 3, 4, 7

 Do I ...?

1. Do I have clear aims?

   Yes ☐ **No** ☐

2. Do I have a sense of what might prevent me from completing the course?

   Yes ☐ **No** ☐

3. Do I have a sense of what might prevent me getting most from this experience?

   Yes ☐ **No** ☐

4. Do I have realistic ideas about how I will manage potential problems?

   Yes ☐ **No** ☐

To do. I will ...

Plan towards your success

Consider each of the following, taking action as needed. Check off ✔ each step once completed.

Your aims
What do you want to gain, personally, from your time as an international student? Write it down.

Potential setbacks
Make a list of anything that might get in the way of your success.

Problem-solving
Think about solutions: what will you do to deal with those potential set-backs?

Motivators
If things get tough, what will keep you going? What will inspire you? Write these down.

Make a 20+ list
Increase motivation through a strong list of things to see, do, visit and achieve, on your course, living in a new country or from travel.

'50 Ways'
Identify which ones will help you cope and succeed. Decide when you will use these. Put these in your diary/planner.[36]

Sources of help
At uni or college and through agencies, family and friends.

Make a plan
… to guide and motivate you to achieve your aims.

Find out more
See Cottrell, S. (2019) *The Study Skills Handbook*.[37]

6

Use the right psychology

Success starts in the mind

Do I ...?

1. Do I have good coping strategies?
   Yes ☐ No ☐

2. Do I bring a positive attitude?
   Yes ☐ No ☐

3. Do I have a good sense of humour?
   Yes ☐ No ☐

4. Do I love to learn from experience?
   Yes ☐ No ☐

Why is this important?

All students find life or study hard at times, and being an international student brings additional layers of challenge. Good psychological coping mechanisms help you to get through bad days and add to your happiness and effectiveness. The way students perceive difficulties, and their general attitude to challenges, impact on confidence, self-esteem, stress, health and academic success. Ultimately, it is up to you whether you adopt an attitude that makes you feel better, or worse, about your experiences.

To do. I will ...

Considering your responses

If you can find the humour in most contexts and find useful learning in all aspects of your experience, then every situation brings you something positive. It is useful to develop such an attitude to help you cope when things don't go exactly as planned.

See also Ways 4, 15, 26, 32

Bring a great attitude

Decide ✔ which of the following would be helpful for you to do.

Expect a good time
Be determined to enjoy yourself, learn a lot and create memories, even if not everything is perfect.

Prepare for the worst
... so things are less of a shock if they go wrong. Plan ahead to avoid problems where you can.

Make it fun
Consider it a game or adventure!

Don't assume disaster
Look for a way through. List the things you learn from the problems.

Have a stress strategy
Take steps to manage pressure before it gets too much – see Way 26.[38]

Look for the humour
... even when things go wrong! Imagine telling the story 20 years from now, and finding the funny side.

Inspire yourself
... with your '20+' list (pages 112–13).

Recognise achievement
Take stock of all you have done, learned and accomplished so far. Jot these down in your planner for a ready reminder.[36] Give yourself credit and praise!

7

Sort out 'must-do' actions early

Smooth out your path

? Do I ...?

1. Do I know for certain this is the right course for me – based on thorough research of the country, uni, course and costs?

   Yes ☐ **No** ☐

2. Do I need a visa to study?

   Yes ☐ **No** ☐

3. Am I well organised, making arrangements to ensure everything will go smoothly?

   Yes ☐ **No** ☐

Why is this important?

These 7 actions can have a great impact on the success of your studies. It is important not to commit yourself to a course until you are sure it is the right one, as it can be expensive to change. It might mean waiting a year or paying an additional year's costs. Don't confirm your place until you know you can meet visa and financial requirements. If you plan these 7 actions well, you will start your study abroad with fewer problems and greater enjoyment.

Considering your responses

Consider whether your responses suggest you have any doubts about the decisions you are making. If so, talk to an adviser and think things through carefully. Avoid leaving anything to chance or to the last minute. If your responses indicate that you are not planning things carefully and well in advance, make a schedule of what to do and when to do it.

 See also Ways 8, 9, 10, 11

To do. I will …

Get organised!

Indicate ✔ when you have completed each 'must-do' action.

☐ **Check you can afford it**
Add up all costs including fees, living costs, study costs, travel, etc. Sort your finances first. Don't assume you will find work or scholarships on arrival.

☐ **Confirm your place**
Check the course really is the right one for you. If so, confirm your place and get evidence of this. Without this, you won't be able to get the right visa (if required).

☐ **Sort your visa**
Find out if you need one and, if so, what is required to gain this. For study in the UK, USA or other countries, see page 117.

☐ **Get a bank account**
Check whether there is a bank you can access easily from both home and abroad. If possible, set up an account before you leave home.[39]

☐ **Sort accommodation**
Unless you are staying with friends or family, apply early for this. For your first year, consider a room on campus. Find out what you will need to do to secure accommodation in future years.

☐ **Plan your journey**
Plot your journey from A to B, thinking through what is needed at each stage. Check whether your college or uni arranges for you to be met at the airport or station, and what to do if you arrive at night.

☐ **Get correct insurance**
Check the insurance you will need for loss or damage to belongings whilst away, as well as for travel and health. Look for good student deals.

8

Organise essentials to bring with you

Travel light and smart

Why is this important?

The things you *really* want and need will seem even more important when away from home, so organise these well in advance. Think through what you would find essential for study, sports, music or other interests, as well as to reduce homesickness and ease life abroad. Consider what to carry and what to have delivered to you. Find out what you are allowed to carry and items you can purchase easily or more cheaply after you arrive.

Considering your responses

Consider whether you could be more organised in your planning of what to take. Use electronic storage where possible. Avoid taking items you don't really need or can get when you arrive. Check how much you are allowed to take on board planes, including internal connection flights.

 See also Ways 9, 10, 13, 50

1. Do I know what I am allowed to bring into the countries I study in/visit?

Yes ☐ No ☐

2. Do I have a good checklist of things I will need?

Yes ☐ No ☐

3. Do I want to have any items sent ahead by post?

Yes ☐ No ☐

4. Do I know what I need on arrival?

Yes ☐ No ☐

To do. I will ...

Make life easier

Indicate ✔ when you have organised each item below.

Travel essentials
Make a good checklist of items that you will need (pages 18–21). Check you have these before leaving home.

Items cheaper at home
Compare prices before leaving home, to decide where is best to purchase clothes, shoes, electrical items, cables, apps, etc.

Essential medical items
Check whether it is permitted to bring these into the country. You might need a doctor's letter and/or a prescription.

Dictionary
It can be useful to have a dictionary in your first language as well as the study language.

Things for the journey
Items that will ease a long journey (or any long delays!).

Money – in cash
Bring a range of local coins for machines you might need to use in the airport. Bring money to cover 2–3 nights in a hotel, in case of emergency, and cash for a few weeks, in case of problems with bank accounts.

The right adaptors
Check plugs of electrical items fit sockets of countries where you will be staying. Bring a few adaptors, in case any get left behind in hotels.

A touch of home
Bring items that help you feel more at home whilst away, and things to share at cultural events or with friends.

Items to pack, check or prepare before leaving home

Check these ✔ once packed (or posted).

Add any other items to bring (or post) if not already listed.

Documents/Information

- [ ] Passport
- [ ] Visa
- [ ] Tickets
- [ ] Pre-printed boarding card
- [ ] Any other required proof of ID
- [ ] Travel insurance details
- [ ] Other insurance details
- [ ] Offer letter from uni/college
- [ ] Details of funding or sponsor
- [ ] Details of accommodation

- [ ] Directions and maps to uni
- [ ] Directions to accommodation
- [ ] Campus map
- [ ] Tutor name and contact details
- [ ] Details of main contact at uni
- [ ] Uni's international office details
- [ ] Health certificates
- [ ] Driving licence if you have one
- [ ] Details of your embassy or consulate (for emergencies only)

Other travel essentials:

- [ ]
- [ ]
- [ ]
- [ ]

- [ ]
- [ ]
- [ ]
- [ ]

Health and hygiene

- [ ] Prescription drugs
- [ ] Medical card/documentation
- [ ] Medical insurance
- [ ] Glasses or contact lenses

- [ ] Toiletries
- [ ] Toothbrush
- [ ] Hairbrush

Other health and hygiene items:
- ☐
- ☐

- ☐
- ☐

Money
- ☐ Cash for countries stayed in
- ☐ Coins for machines

- ☐ Cards
- ☐ Bank details/address

Electrical
- ☐ Adaptors
- ☐ Laptop
- ☐ Devices
- ☐ Cables

- ☐ Extension lead
- ☐ Chargers
- ☐ Hairdryer
- ☐ Hair styling equipment

Other electrical items:
- ☐
- ☐
- ☐

- ☐
- ☐
- ☐

Taste of home
- ☐ Photos
- ☐ Small gifts
- ☐ Chocolate/sweets
- ☐ Recipes/cookbook
- ☐ Seasoning/spices/sauces*

- ☐ Music
- ☐ Personal items
- ☐ Contact details for friends
- ☐ Information saved to phone/device

Other 'taste of home' items:
- ☐
- ☐
- ☐
- ☐

- ☐
- ☐
- ☐
- ☐

* Subject to any travel restrictions

Music

- ☐ Downloaded music
- ☐ Playlists
- ☐ Instruments
- ☐ Sheet music

Other music-related items:

- ☐
- ☐
- ☐
- ☐

Sports/leisure

- ☐
- ☐
- ☐
- ☐
- ☐
- ☐
- ☐
- ☐

Clothes

- ☐ Coat
- ☐ Jacket
- ☐ Clothes for formal occasions
- ☐ Clothes for travelling
- ☐ Clothes for weather on arrival
- ☐ Sport-related clothing
- ☐
- ☐
- ☐
- ☐
- ☐
- ☐
- ☐
- ☐
- ☐
- ☐
- ☐
- ☐
- ☐
- ☐

Shoes/footwear

- ☐ Shoes 1:
- ☐ Shoes 2:
- ☐ Shoes 3:
- ☐

Study-related

- [ ] Info sent by uni/college
- [ ] Dictionary or language apps
- [ ] Relevant notes
- [ ] Book:

- [ ] Book:
- [ ] Book:
- [ ] Book:
- [ ] Book:

Other study related items:
- [ ]
- [ ]
- [ ]

- [ ]
- [ ]
- [ ]

Other items

- [ ]
- [ ]
- [ ]
- [ ]
- [ ]

- [ ]
- [ ]
- [ ]
- [ ]
- [ ]

Things for the journey

- [ ] Eye-mask
- [ ] Headphones
- [ ] Playlist
- [ ] Snacks
- [ ] Change of footwear
- [ ] Toothbrush
- [ ] Book
- [ ] Phone
- [ ]
- [ ]
- [ ]
- [ ]

- [ ]
- [ ]
- [ ]
- [ ]
- [ ]
- [ ]
- [ ]
- [ ]

9 Research what to buy once abroad

Make student life easier and cheaper

1. Do I know what I need for my course?
   Yes ☐ **No** ☐

2. Do I know what will be provided free by the course or university?
   Yes ☐ **No** ☐

3. Do I know what might be available cheaper with a student card?
   Yes ☐ **No** ☐

4. Do I know what is cheaper, or easy to buy, in the country of study?
   Yes ☐ **No** ☐

Why is this important?

It is useful to research what it will be possible to buy once in the host country, either in shops near the university or college or online. Check whether attitudes towards haggling are similar to those at home. Compare prices. You can then choose what to buy in advance or on arrival so you have everything you need at the best price and by the most convenient method. This can save you money, and might help you travel lighter.

Considering your responses

Give thought to whether your responses show you really know what you need for study and life at uni or college in the host country. A little more research might make life as a student much easier. Items listed opposite can make a big difference. Consider what else might be of practical use to you – such as for socialising, cooking or travelling locally.

 See also Ways 8, 10, 16, 22

To do. I will …

Useful initial purchases

Indicate ✔ when you have considered each item below.

☐ **Extension lead**
1–2 of these will mean you can use more of your electrical items.

☐ **Clothes for local weather**
Check where local people go for bargain clothes, shoes and coats.

☐ **Student card**
Good for discounts on travel, eating out and other items. Student organisations and support services at your uni or college can usually advise on these.

☐ **TV licence**
If watching TV programmes on a device or phone, you might need your own licence. Check this out for the country where you study.

☐ **HDMI cable**
Use to watch videos/programmes streamed or downloaded via your phone to a TV screen – great for nights in with friends.

☐ **Ear plugs and eye-mask**
Useful for getting sleep whenever you need to fit it in, when travelling or in student accommodation.

☐ **Essential text books**
These may be cheaper on campus or in local bookshops. Check what is available through the university or college library first.

☐ **Slippers and bathrobe**
Get footwear and robes that are easy to wear for fire drills, travel, using the bathroom, answering the door and relaxing after a bath.

10

Be moneywise

Keep finances under control

Why is this important?

Financial difficulty affects many students. It causes stress and is often the reason why students leave before finishing their course. Problems stem from multiple and diverse causes: unexpected changes in currency exchange rates; assuming there will be work available but finding there is not; spending too much money in the first few weeks; and not realising how much it costs to purchase some frequently used and everyday items. Keeping your finances under control can make a big difference to your success.

Considering your responses

If your responses suggest that you are not fully in control of your finances, take steps straight away to organise these. Check your spending habits and your accounts frequently. Don't take risks with your money. Speak to student advice services early, to help avoid problems.

(i) Find out more

The Macmillan Student Planner is good for financial planning, with annually updated information about sites and apps to help save money.

 Do I ...?

1. Do I monitor my income, costs and finances carefully and often?

Yes ☐ No ☐

2. Do I know how to make a little money go a long way?

Yes ☐ No ☐

3. Do I have a good sense of what things cost?

Yes ☐ No ☐

4. Do I watch the exchange rates?

Yes ☐ No ☐

 See also

Ways 7, 8, 9, 49

 To do. I will ...

Enjoy a bargain

Indicate ✔ which of the following could be useful for you to do.

Get the right banking
Research well. Get the right account for you as an international student.

Learn the exchange rates
Use them to monitor your money and the best times to exchange it.

Know your bank balance
Check frequently how much money you have in your account.

Budget for essentials
Keep a separate account for fees, bills and other essentials. Don't use this for anything else.

Monitor your spend
List what you buy and what it costs. Know how much you spend – so there are no horrible surprises! *The Macmillan Student Planner* can help with this.[36]

Find out about bargains
Use websites and apps for cheaper prices. Find out where local people go for a good deal when eating out or shopping. Be aware of how to haggle in each country you visit.

Use financial help at uni
Visit support services for financial workshops, tips and advice.

Learn to cook
... save money and treat friends!

11 Attend welcome events

... for a great way to settle in

Why is this important?

Social and cultural integration have been identified as key issues for success as an international student.[11,40] Welcome events are designed to help you settle in as quickly and easily as possible. They provide an ideal opportunity to meet people and gain important information,[12] and they can be highly enjoyable. They usually provide a quick overview of key aspects of student life, facilities and support. Follow these up in more detail later.

Considering your responses

If you hadn't planned to attend such events, it is worth doing so, even if it means arriving early, or costs you more. These events, as well as providing extra time to spend settling into life and studying before term begins, can make a great difference to your study and well-being in the year ahead.[41, 42]

1. Do I know the dates and times of welcome events?

    Yes   **No**

2. Do my travel plans enable me to attend all the welcome events?

    Yes   **No**

3. Do I know if my uni/college runs special events for international students?

    Yes   **No**

4. Do I feel confident about attending such events?

    Yes   **No**

 To do. I will ...

 See also Ways 12, 14, 16, 18, 19

Join in! Meet others! Get informed!

Attend international student events

Great for gaining essential information and practical advice as well as meeting other international students. They are often held before other students arrive, so you get a chance to settle in first.

Attend freshers' week

Find out about the huge range of student events, sports, clubs and societies on offer. A good way to meet other students, most of whom will be looking to make new friends.

Attend course events

… for students in your faculty, department or on your course. Make them a priority. Use them to find out about your course and to meet classmates and tutors.

Join clubs and societies

Go to the first meetings – you will then feel more comfortable attending future meetings. You don't have to be an expert to join these – just have fun!

Prioritise information

Don't worry about remembering all the information you receive. Flag what is essential for the next few days ahead. File everything. Sort through it over the next two weeks.

12 Bond with your university

Gain a sense of belonging

 Do I ...?

1. Do I want to feel a greater sense of belonging at my college/uni?

Yes ☐ **No** ☐

2. Do I feel proud of being a student here?
Yes ☐ **No** ☐

3. Do I do anything to contribute to the sense of community?

Yes ☐ **No** ☐

Why is this important?

A study of international students at eight universities in the USA in 2014 found that when international students had a sense of 'belonging', they mixed more across cultures and gained much better grades.[42] Taking part in leadership programmes, helping out in the community and attending cultural events were especially effective in helping students feel they belong. Engaging in extra-curricular activity can bring all-round benefit to life and academic study.[43]

Considering your responses

If you already feel a strong sense of belonging to your institution, that is good. If not, taking action to nurture this can be important to your long-term success. What leads to a sense of belonging is highly personal so if the methods given opposite don't appeal, be creative in finding other ways of connecting to people and your university or college.

 To do. I will ...

 See also Ways 11, 14, 15, 31, 47

Help forge a vibrant student community

Leadership programmes

Look for programmes run by Careers and Employability Services, enterprise or entrepreneurship schemes, or through the business school. Find out what courses are available.

Help out on campus

Giving something of yourself helps to create connections. Helping out is a good way to meet people and become known to others. You can also get better informed about your institution and develop new skills – plus helping others can make your time meaningful.

Cultural events

Attending events such as concerts, art exhibitions, speaker events, meals or international student events provides a chance for you to link up with friends, meet new people and share experiences. These provide a good starting point for future conversations.

Celebrate its successes

Take part in events such as shows, matches, quizzes, competitions. Support it in competitive events. Help organise supporter events, or run competitions on campus. Talk to others about what your college/ uni does well, whatever that might be.

Contribute to student life

Look for other ways of contributing to student life – take part in the sports, suggest an event, offer to help students who need it. Ask Student Services, Careers and the Student Union/Student Guild about the options.

13

Combat homesickness

Don't let homesickness win!

1. Do I miss home a lot?

Yes ☐ No ☐

2. Do I feel I don't fit in here?

Yes ☐ No ☐

3. Do I feel sad or lonely?

Yes ☐ No ☐

4. Do I often feel like leaving?

Yes ☐ No ☐

Why is this important?

It is natural to miss people and places and to feel homesick when in a new place, especially if much is unfamiliar.[20] Homesickness can lead to stress and undermine confidence – it affects students academically, too.[44,45,46,47] Most students experience this to some extent, whether home or international.[48,49] It is important not to rush home at every opportunity or give up on the experience. Instead, give yourself time to acclimatise to your new surroundings and form new bonds. Joining in with others and creating your own space helps you to make a new home away from home.

Considering your responses

If your responses suggest that homesickness might get in the way of your success, don't let this happen. Homesickness will reduce or mostly go away. Treat yourself to small tastes of home from time to time, but focus on being in the now and becoming familiar with a new place.

To do. I will ...

 See also Ways 8, 14, 18, 19

Create a new 'home' away from home

Indicate ✔ which might be useful for you to try!

Create a 'home corner'
Dedicate part of your room for relaxing with photos, music and a few items from home.

The aroma of home
Bring some soap, cosmetics, spices and similar items. Use sparingly, so they don't run out.

Toothpaste and brush
Bring these from home as familiar objects you use everyday.

Stay active
Distract yourself. Get out of your room when not studying or resting.

Create a new routine
Make a schedule. Find places you like on campus or nearby. Visit these every day until you settle in.

Build familiarity
For a while, sit in the same seat in lectures and in the library to study. These will give you a location that feels more familiar – and others will get used to seeing you, too.

Skype home occasionally
Plan it ahead as a treat. Show and talk about photos so friends/family share your experience.

Discuss your experience
Talking about cultural differences with international students helps reduce homesickness.[24]

Join in!
Become part of a new crowd. Let others get to know you. Bond more with them at uni/college.

14

Get socialising!

Make opportunities to link and meet

Why is this important?

The first students you meet won't necessarily be those with whom you become closest friends. They might change to new classes or drift to other friends. It is important to form a wide network of acquaintances. They won't all be friends, but one link leads to another quickly in student circles, and there will be some with whom you form deeper connections. Such networks can make it easier to find others for support, study groups and team projects. They open up new opportunities for friendships, trips, food and contacts useful for your future.

Considering your responses

If your responses suggest that you don't feel confident about networking, or are not sure how, then don't worry. Just attend a lot of different events and be open to meeting people. Consider your list of 20+ (pages 112–13): do your networks help you to achieve this? If not, find out where you can meet people who share your interests or who can help you.

 See also Ways 11, 12, 18, 19, 48

 Do I ...?

1. Do I know how to network?

   Yes ☐   **No** ☐

2. Do I feel confident networking?

   Yes ☐   **No** ☐

3. Do I make an effort to network?

   Yes ☐   **No** ☐

4. Do I mix with a wide variety of people from uni and elsewhere?

   Yes ☐   **No** ☐

 To do. I will ...

Be active in forming networks!

Be first to smile and speak

Don't assume that others won't want to talk to you.

Show an interest in others

Ask them about their lives, family, study, career plans, travel, music – or anything that interests you.

Sign up for a mentor

Most colleges/unis have mentor or buddy schemes: existing students show you round, and share tips and experiences.

Attend events and parties

Take advantage of the wide range of events, films, music, guest speakers, parties, career-related events, and much more.

Join in and turn up

… even if it feels difficult or frustrating. Other people will also be shy or anxious about meeting strangers (even if they don't look it!), so it might take time for everyone to relax, get used to each other and 'be themselves'.

Join student societies

A great aspect of student life and a lifeline for international students.[12,18,28]

Start your own society

If you don't find a student society that suits you, start your own! Ask your student union or guild about how to get started.

Go on excursions and trips

… or organise one yourself. As well as seeing more of the country, it helps build networks.

15

Enjoy the cultural variety

Cultivate a spirit of adventure

Why is this important?

International study offers the chance to experience the host culture in depth, which can be fun and enjoyable if you are open to it.[12,13,28,50] Be prepared to be surprised, amazed, baffled, shocked and entertained even in countries that share a common language or history.[27] Look out for similarities, too! As a student, you have exceptional opportunities for getting to know people from around the world and finding out how and why cultures vary. This can be useful, too, as cultural awareness is an asset to many jobs and careers.

Considering your responses

Consider whether your responses show you are making the most of this opportunity to learn about, and enjoy, cultural differences. Remember that employers worldwide need graduates who are culturally sensitive.

 See also Ways 18, 24, 29, 49

1. Do I enjoy being with people from different countries?

    Yes   No

2. Do I like trying food from different countries?

    Yes   No

3. Do I live in the same way as local people whilst away from home?

    Yes   No

4. Do I find out why people think and do things differently elsewhere?

    Yes   No

 To do. I will …

Respect the difference!

Broaden your experience
Be politely curious. Try out things you couldn't find elsewhere.[12,51]

Look for the positives
Find the fun and interest in cultural difference. Enjoy the pleasure of discovering new things, even if some seem strange to you.[12,13]

Understand difference
Discover how and why things differ to back home. Show interest.

Be present in the moment
Don't focus on what you think is wrong or missing compared to back home – immerse yourself in the new experiences.

Gain cultural competence
Develop skills and knowledge relevant to future work and life.[37,52]

Be respectful
Avoid criticising other people for thinking and doing things differently in their countries. Even if people criticise their own culture, they generally don't like others to do so!

Enrich your future life
Look for new ways of thinking, being and doing things that you would like to continue once you return home. Collect recipes, playlists and skills to take home.

16

Make your own survival guide

Essential information at a glance

Do I ...?

1. Do I have lots of new information to remember?

   Yes ☐ **No** ☐

2. Do I have to keep checking to find this in different places or sites?

   Yes ☐ **No** ☐

3. Do I waste time trying to find out where I saw information or where I stored it?

   Yes ☐ **No** ☐

Why is this important?

As an international student, there is usually a great deal to remember about how everything operates. Take the effort out of remembering it; keep it all in one place, by creating your own survival guide. Build this as you go along, whenever you need to check things out. Create sections relevant for you, such as using new appliances, purchasing tickets, documentation you need to carry, where to find food you enjoy, aspects of the law that are useful to know, cultural expectations and signs of politeness that differ to your own country.

Considering your responses

Consider whether you are storing potentially useful information as effectively as you might. If not, create your own guide, either in a light notebook that fits easily in your bag or on a device or phone. Alternatively, keep it in a student planner/diary.[36]

 To do. I will ...

 See also Ways 10, 17, 22, 26

Personalise your survival guide

Academic	Travel
<ul><li>Differences to note in what is expected of you</li><li>Vocabulary and phrases</li><li>Useful study tips, apps, etc.</li><li>Essential dates</li><li>Names of tutors and classmates.</li></ul>	<ul><li>Travel tips</li><li>Places to visit</li><li>Short cuts to new places</li><li>How to purchase tickets for trains, coaches, buses</li><li>Useful phrases for travel.</li></ul>
Life	**Advice to self**
<ul><li>Cheap places to buy things</li><li>Good places to eat</li><li>Tips on finances and ways to make or save money</li><li>How to use appliances: the cooker, oven, washing machine and dryers</li><li>Recipes for meals you like</li><li>How to apply for a work visa</li><li>Tips on applying for jobs or voluntary work.</li></ul>	<ul><li>Which documents to bring</li><li>Motivational tips</li><li>Things you want to remember to take home</li><li>Things to do before going home</li><li>Reminders of birthdays and special occasions.</li></ul>

17 Create your own active phrase book

Collect words and phrases relevant to you

? Do I ...?

1. Do I listen out for new phrases?

   Yes ☐ No ☐

2. Do I learn them and their usage, so I can use them correctly?

   Yes ☐ No ☐

3. Do I keep a record of useful new words and phrases so I can find them easily?

   Yes ☐ No ☐

Why is this important?

When learning a new language, nothing compares to learning it whilst studying abroad. You have excellent opportunities to capture new vocabulary and phrases. It is easy to lose or forget these, so capture them as soon as you see or hear them. Carry a notebook to write them down at speed, or capture them on your device or phone. Either store every phrase alphabetically or create themed sections. Put some time aside every day to review and practise new phrases whilst they are still fresh in your mind.

Considering your responses

Consider whether your responses suggest you would benefit from being more systematic in learning new aspects of the language. You can use dictionaries and apps, but you are more likely to find and use phrases that you have 'made your own' as part of your own active phrase book.

 See also Ways 20, 21, 23, 25, 32

 To do. I will ...

Be systematic in writing down new words and phrases

Specialist vocabulary
Make a habit of writing down technical terms and specialist vocabulary relevant to your subject. Write down their meaning in both the study language and your own.

Academic expressions
Make a note of the ways that ideas are expressed in your subject.

Grammar
Look out for ways that grammar is used, especially in academic texts and in recorded lectures. Keep a record of new grammar, checking with a friend or language tutor that you have understood it correctly. Get an advanced grammar book and learn or revise a small point of grammar every day.

Songs, poems, quotations
These can be easier to learn and remember so a good way of learning new phrases. They can provide interesting alternative ways of expressing thoughts.

Everyday phrases
Ask friends to repeat phrases that you hear on TV, in films, or that you hear them using. Ask them to check you are writing these down accurately, and pronouncing them correctly. Check *when* it is correct to use the expression – and when it isn't. Note pronunciation tips.

18

Connect to other international students

Gain a sense of solidarity

 Do I ...?

1. Do I mix with other international students?

   Yes ☐ No ☐

2. Do I speak in the language of study when with other international students?

   Yes ☐ No ☐

3. Do I help organise social events?

   Yes ☐ No ☐

4. Do I share tips and skills?

   Yes ☐ No ☐

Why is this important?

Spending time with other international students rather than just 'home' students is important for sharing relevant anecdotes, information, tips, phrases, and for recognising similarities in your experiences.[24,53] It can reduce isolation and homesickness, broaden your outlook and boost confidence. It can also help alleviate the stress of culture clash or of being in a minority culture for the first time.[54,55] It is a superb way of building an international network of friends and acquaintances – which might be there for life.

Considering your responses

Consider whether your responses suggest you make the most of socialising and learning with other international students. Whilst it would be limiting to spend all of your time with other international students, it can be good to spend time with people who share similar experiences.

To do. I will ...

 See also Ways 18, 21, 26, 29, 49

Share experience

Gain a sense of solidarity

Offer and receive support and understanding from students with experiences similar to your own.[24,56,57]

Share tips

... about travel, bargains, coping strategies, studying, language, places to see, and surviving whilst living and studying away from home.[58]

Use the language of study

... even when relaxing. Agree to correct each other's mistakes.

Contribute

Take a lead in arranging things to do – whether meeting for breakfast or organising a trip. It develops confidence and leadership skills and builds your CV, too!

Use dedicated spaces

Many unis now provide space or events for international students to meet. Contribute to making these lively places to go. If none is provided, ask student services for help creating separate space and events for international students to meet and support each other.

Bridge language divides

... by sharing photos, helping each other edit and enhance these, and taking group photos.[22] Learn new phrases that express interest in other people's photos.

19

Create wide social networks

Learn more about your host country

Do I ...?

1. Do I mix with 'home' students?

   Yes ☐ No ☐

2. Do I find ways of making connections with 'home' students?

   Yes ☐ No ☐

3. Do I interact with local people?

   Yes ☐ No ☐

4. Do I take steps to meet people in this country apart from students?

   Yes ☐ No ☐

Why is this important?

Many studies show that international students adjust better and are more successful if they have good networks with host-national students as well as spending some time with international students and students from their own culture.[59,60,61,62,63] You also gain a richer experience and learn more about the culture, language and thought processes of the country of study. The International Student Barometer[64] (page 114) indicates that this can make you a happier student too!

Considering your responses

If your responses suggest you are not mixing much with local people and native speakers, then you could be missing out on the international experience. If it feels daunting, pair up with another student to investigate opportunities off-campus or to involve home students in social interactions.

To do. I will …

 See also Ways 18, 24, 29, 46, 48

Broaden your circle

Study in mixed groups

Choose to work with a mix of home and international students for study groups, projects, field trips, etc.

Socialise before/ after class

Make time to chat with home students. Suggest going for coffee, a meal or seeing an exhibition at these times.

Share your language

If the uni teaches your language, offer time for conversation with home students. Alternate using your own and the 'home' language.

Become a 'regular'

When you find a shop, café or place you enjoy, visit it frequently at the same times so people get used to you in their daily lives.

Share your favourite meal

Invite a mix of students or other people you get to know to eat at a restaurant (if possible), or cook a dish from home yourself!

Live with a family

Learn the language as it is spoken. Experience real life in the country you are visiting.[27]

Attend local events

Find out about festivals, sports, volunteering, arts, religious activities or jobs (if you are eligible) for ways to meet local people.[28]

20 Fine-tune your language skills

Express your ideas and understanding well

Why is this important?

For almost all programmes of study, you have a better experience of study and gain better grades if you are fluent in the language of study.[65] Even domestic students need to adapt and refine their use of language to suit the level of study and the styles in which ideas are discussed in their specialist subjects. Greater language proficiency means you comprehend new material more quickly, and can demonstrate more precisely what you have learned. It also builds confidence and can open up opportunities, socially and for jobs.

Considering your responses

If your responses suggest you are not doing enough to improve your language skills, for better communication, fluency and grades, then decide which action to take. What would best motivate and help you to do so?

 See also Ways 17, 23, 25, 30, 32

 Do I ...?

1. Do I work hard at improving my academic language skills?

   Yes ☐ No ☐

2. Am I fluent in the language of study?

   Yes ☐ No ☐

3. Do I know which aspects of language I need to improve to get better grades?

   Yes ☐ No ☐

4. Do I have effective strategies for improving my language skills?

   Yes ☐ No ☐

 To do. I will ...

Develop your fluency

Indicate ✔ which might be useful for you to try!

Spend 20+ minutes a day
… learning new expressions, grammar, pronunciation and application. Vary learning with classes, books, apps, games, videos, chat and your personal phrase book. Over time, this adds up to a lot of learning.

Use available classes
Make full use of classes provided. Even if they seem easy, you can reinforce understanding, improve pronunciation and expression.

Find a language partner
Find a home student interested in conversation in your language. Agree times to meet to talk in each language at least once a week.

Form a study group
Discuss the issues arising from lectures and reading. It helps you learn, remember and develop language – and makes it more fun learning course material.

Watch TV – with subtitles
Watch films, documentaries, videos, live news, chat-shows and a variety of programmes. Listen along as you read the subtitles. You'll start to pick up a wide range of expressions and become familiar with different accents, as well as having something to talk about!

21

Handle classes in a foreign language

Develop the right study habits

? Do I ...?

1. Do I find class-time difficult?

   Yes ☐ **No** ☐

2. Do I prepare well before class?

   Yes ☐ **No** ☐

3. Do I miss information in class?

   Yes ☐ **No** ☐

4. Do I check after class that I have captured all the material correctly?

   Yes ☐ **No** ☐

Why is this important?

If you are not fluent in the language, prepare well before class. Take care to avoid distractions during class, so you can pay close attention throughout. Follow up carefully afterwards on anything you didn't fully understand. Be mindful that language may be used differently when discussing academic topics – typically more formal, precise and specialised. Capture useful expressions in your phrase book and practise them (see Way 17). Lecturers usually provide background notes as starting points; if so, use these as the basis for creating and developing your own notes.

Considering your responses

If your responses suggest that you find class-time hard, don't despair. You may need to rely more on the learning that you do before and after class, so just be prepared for that. Class time is still important. As well as developing your language awareness, it gives you a general feel for the course and material to investigate, as well as maintaining contacts.

To do. I will ...

See also Ways 30, 33, 36, 46

Prepare, listen, refine

Prepare for class

This is good for all students but essential if studying in a foreign language. Read or browse the topic of the lecture before class, or watch a podcast or video. Make some notes. Use class to reinforce your understanding and to improve listening skills.

Listen to recorded lectures and podcasts after class

Listen to the best lectures several times, to learn the topic. Pick up on any material missed in class, and with less stress. Gain familiarity with how language is used for topics you are studying.

Write and say

Write down specialist terms and other new vocabulary, and their meaning. Speak these aloud so your ear becomes more familiar with them before class. Practise answering responses to questions you could be asked.

Refine your notes

Make a few notes to prepare for lectures. After class, use notes, recordings, podcasts or reading to add to these – make sure you cover all the important points. (See Way 22.)

Focus on listening in class

Sit where you can see and hear well, with least distraction from others. Avoid multi-tasking – keep listening even if you don't understand much.

Time

It can take much longer to study in a foreign language so it is essential to plan and use time carefully. (See Way 34.)

22

Adapt your study skills

... relevant to the country and level of study

 Do I ...?

1. Do I have study strategies relevant to my course?

    Yes ☐   No ☐

2. Do I know what is different about requirements at each level of study?

    Yes ☐   No ☐

3. Do I know the areas where I need to improve my skills?

    Yes ☐   No ☐

Why is this important?

Whether studying at home or abroad, it is wise to review, adapt and enhance your study skills in ways relevant to the course, country and level of study. Each year, the level of difficulty increases, so your levels of knowledge, skills and understanding need to increase, too. Adapting and upgrading your study skills is useful even if you have performed well in the past – but even more so if you haven't always received the grades you wanted.

Considering your responses

If your responses suggest you haven't reviewed, adapted and upgraded your study skills recently, doing so would be a useful step towards success. It can boost confidence to be clearer about what is expected, where your strengths lie and where to improve further.

 Find out more

See Cottrell, S. (2019). *The Study Skills Handbook* as a starting place. See page 116.

 See also Ways 27, 34, 38, 39, 45

 To do. I will ...

Keep sharpening your academic skills

Review your study skills

Be more aware of the underlying skills, habits and attitudes that impact on your time, effectiveness and grades.

Know your study strengths

Use these to guide your choice of topics and assignments.

Improve in your weak areas

Focus on improving those which will have most impact.

Be aware of the differences

… from your previous courses and for each year of study. Use course handbooks and assessment criteria to find out what is expected. Consider carefully the implications for your own study and language skills: how will you need to adapt these?

Ask to see examples

Your tutors or the library might be able to provide examples of good assignments, so you can see the standard expected.

23

Learn local idiom

Understand the varieties of language use

1. Do I enjoy talking to local people?

Yes ☐ No ☐

2. Do I want to know different ways the language is used?

Yes ☐ No ☐

3. Do I want to sound 'local'?

Yes ☐ No ☐

4. Do I want to understand what is meant when idiom is used in various media?

Yes ☐ No ☐

Why is this important?

Feel more at home in a country through building an association with one or more of its regions. Local people will often be pleased (or amused!) that you use local phrases. It creates openings for conversations: you can ask about whether you pronounced or used expressions correctly. It also suggests to local people that you are more settled in the area rather than just a passing tourist, making them more likely to take a kind interest in you.

Considering your responses

If you want to fit into the local community, or just understand more of what is being said, then it is good to learn local dialects and idiom. This can be fun to do and means you can pick up expressions when used in other media too. It is a good way of learning about language, and helps you develop an ear for where people come from, regionally and socially.

 To do. I will ...

 See also Ways 24, 25, 32, 41

Be mistaken for 'a local'

Learn common sayings As a starting place, check online for idiom and expressions used in the host country.[66,67]

Note local expressions Jot these down in your personal phrase book (see Way 17).

Get the sound just right When using idiom, practise getting the pacing, accent, intonation and phrasing perfect. Otherwise, it can sound odd.

Surprise the 'locals' You will sound very 'at home' in the language if you get local idiom right.

Find out when to use it … and also when not to. Incorrect use can be confusing or a sign of disrespect. Learn the nuanced use of idiom.

Attend local events so you get to hear more regional accents.

Not for academic work Usually, idiom is for everyday use rather than formal, academic use.

Listen for it in the media If you understand local idiom, even mainstream media will probably make more sense. Listen out for expressions you have heard before or learned already.

24 Volunteer in the community

... lend a helping hand!

Why is this important?

Volunteering is popular amongst international students. It is good for community spirit. You contribute to helping others, find out about the culture, gain new experiences and even travel and socialise at little or no cost. You mix with people you might not meet otherwise. In addition, you can develop useful skills and attributes such as problem-solving, organising, responsibility, cultural sensitivity and teamwork. These are good for confidence and your CV. If your visa does not permit paid work, volunteering is one way of developing skills and qualities useful to future employment.

Considering your responses

If you want to feel useful, meet people, gain skills and broaden your experience, then volunteering in the local community could be right for you. Decide whether you wish to make a regular commitment, lead a project or just help out occasionally when needed.

 See also Ways 19, 23, 32, 42

? Do I ...?

1. Do I want to meet new people?

   Yes ☐ No ☐

2. Do I enjoy helping others?

   Yes ☐ No ☐

3. Do I want to develop new skills?

   Yes ☐ No ☐

4. Do I want to feel useful?

   Yes ☐ No ☐

 To do. I will ...

Widen your horizons by helping others

Find out what students say

Check uni websites to find out what other students have done, what they learned and enjoyed about it, and what they recommend.

Check your visa

Make sure you are allowed to do unpaid work, and how many hours. Only do what is permitted and ask for advice if you are not sure.

Check the opportunities

Your uni/college, student union or guild, and community and religious groups are all useful sources.

Decide where to volunteer

There are usually opportunities on campus, locally, nationally or internationally.

Design your own project

If your uni helps to fund volunteering projects, suggest a project that interests you.

Offer to lead a project

Gain more skills and responsibility – and great for your CV! Find out about any regulations that might apply and whether there is funding available to cover costs.

25 Use media like the locals

... think and talk like the locals!

Why is this important?

The varied media used in each country provide an excellent way of learning the language as used in everyday life. This will be quite distinct from language used in books and lectures. Notice the different expressions used across the various media, the frequency that certain phrases are used, and how groups of words are pronounced when spoken at speed. You also gain insights into culture – the topics, events, issues and celebrities that influence thinking. Using local media helps you to understand references that are made to characters and stories within everyday speech.

Considering your responses

If you don't make much use of the diverse local media, then do consider the opportunity whilst in the country. Many are available free or at low cost. It is easier to understand the language if you are familiar with varied accents, colloquial usage and cultural references.

 See also Ways 20, 23, 32, 41

 Do I ...?

1. Do I use varied local media?

   Yes ☐ No ☐

2. Do I know what is popular currently in the home student community?

   Yes ☐ No ☐

3. Do I know which TV channels or programmes offer subtitles?

   Yes ☐ No ☐

 To do. I will ...

Broaden your range of cultural references

Children's TV and books Find out words learned by natives as part of their language history – speech patterns vary by age.

Audio books Listen to a chapter before sleeping, or when travelling. Select a range, classic and more recent, to gain a broader familiarity with the culture.

Magazines Great for colloquial language. Browse them in shops or stations for new phrases. Buy a specialist magazine in areas such as science, fashion or IT.

Advertisements Useful as they repeat phrases and are designed to be easy to remember. Good reminders of grammar or vocabulary.

TV, video, films, soaps Follow spoken language using subtitles if available. See which phrases you can recognise and repeat.

Radio and quiz shows Good for making you listen carefully to what is said and learning to understand at speed.

26

Get ahead of stress

Take steps to avoid excess stress

Why is this important?

Most students feel over-stressed at times.[38,68] There are additional pressures for international students. Language barriers, cultural differences and even discrimination can add to stress, making it harder to settle in, make firm friendships and cope with study. Continued stress can affect health, happiness, sleep, social life, decision-making, academic grades and course completion.[32,33,63,69,70] Often, international students blame themselves. They don't want to burden others so try to sort out problems alone.[34,63,70] That is hard, so good strategies and social networks are then especially important.

Considering your responses

If you are feeling over-stressed by the pressures of your situation, don't suffer alone. Many students (and staff) will recognise what you are going through. Find out about ways to prevent or reduce excess stress. Student services can offer good guidance or help you to find other sources of support.

See also Ways 6, 13, 14, 18, 37

> **(?) Do I ...?**
>
> **1.** Do I get very stressed at times?
>
>   Yes ☐ No ☐
>
> **2.** Do I talk to anyone about this?
>
>   Yes ☐ No ☐
>
> **3.** Do I know how to reduce stress?
>
>   Yes ☐ No ☐
>
> **4.** Would I ask support services for help with stress and anxiety?
>
>   Yes ☐ No ☐

> **To do. I will ...**

Find healthy ways to cope

Talk to others

… about your experience, whether family, friends, tutors or student services. It helps you cope with the pressure and to find solutions.

Widen your social network

Being with a mix of international and home students helps to prevent stress.[63]

Use expert support

If there are counselling services, you are not a burden to them and they are used to dealing with a very wide range of student stress.

Improve language skills

Better language skills are associated with lower levels of stress.[71,72]

Spend time with others

Being around others from your own or similar cultures can help, especially if it is not typical to talk about difficulties in your culture.[55]

Use good coping strategies

There are lots of healthy and fun ways to use, reduce and manage stress and cope with pressure.[38,73]

Be kind to yourself

Avoid coping mechanisms such as self-blame, self-harm, self-neglect or substance abuse. Take care of your general health and well-being.

Find a mentor

These can be great for tips and helpful chats. Decide whether you would prefer one from your own culture (see Way 46).

27

Apply your study wisdom!

You know it – so do it!

Why is this important?

Most students have a good internal understanding of what they can do to improve their grades, at least to a certain extent. They also have a good idea of how to avoid catastrophe. If you follow your internal good sense, you will avoid a great deal of stress and difficulty. Opposite are some obvious ways of staying on top of your studies. Add, and stick to, others you know would make a difference for you. You have study wisdom, but it is important to actually use it!

Considering your responses

If you act in ways you *know* are not helpful, this suggests you can also find ways to apply your own wisdom. Consider what prevents you from following your own best advice. It might be peer pressure, loneliness, lack of confidence or many other reasons. If you can't sort that out on your own, talk to a study counsellor so you get back on track quickly.

 See also Ways 22, 34, 39, 46

(?) Do I ...?

1. Do I keep myself well organised?

   Yes **No**

2. Do I follow through on things I know I need to do?

   Yes **No**

3. Do I keep my study in balance with other aspects of my life?

   Yes **No**

4. Do I apply my study wisdom?

   Yes **No**

To do. I will ...

Stir your wise owl!

Work/life balance

Balance your hard work with rest, social life, exercise and sleep.

Tell yourself what to do!

Give yourself praise or a pep talk when needed.

Keep studies on track

Don't get behind – it means more work to do later on. Make a realistic study schedule and use it.

Attend all classes

… even if not a requirement. Don't be late! Don't leave early! It is the best way of knowing you have missed nothing important.

Focus when in class

… it means less work later.

Value your autonomy

Recognise that you are in charge of much of your study time in higher education. Use it well.[37,74]

Party – but not all the time

After welcome week, reduce partying to around once a week.

Get super-organised

… to feel more confident, less stressed, waste less time and have more time for fun and fine-tuning your work.[37,74]

Get assessment right

Avoid gaining lower grades just because of submitting work late or not using the guidance. Know and follow the rules and regulations.

28

Blog it!

Enjoy being part of a blogging community

Why is this important?

Writing and reading blogs bring many benefits including improved thinking and language skills.[75] These connect you to other students, reducing isolation. You can use them to include friends and family at home in your experience, and also to create a great record of your time abroad to look at when you return home. Blogging can help you to organise your thoughts and shape your opinions – useful before starting an assignment. Your university or college might host blogs for free or be able to advise on free hosts and security when using them.

Considering your responses

If you are not keeping a regular blog already, have a go. Decide whether you want this to be mainly for you, or for sharing with family, friends, students, or to be open to anyone. Write about things that interest you and write in your own style. Read and comment on others' blogs too, for inspiration and social connection.

 See also Ways 14, 18, 30, 36

 Do I ...?

1. Do I maintain a regular blog?

Yes ☐ No ☐

2. Do I read other people's blogs?

Yes ☐ No ☐

3. Do I comment on blogs?

Yes ☐ No ☐

4. Do I use blogs to help my study?

Yes ☐ No ☐

 Find out more

See page 117, 'Writing a blog'.

 To do. I will ...

Explore your thoughts

Find a voice
… express your thoughts.
Write about what interests or helps you.

Create a good record
… of your experiences and ideas. Include photos for a richer record
and to engage your readers.

Invite and make comments
… to involve others and learn more.

Blog about your country
… its news, media, music or TV, to maintain links with home.

Blog about your course
… to remember and understand what you read and to explore your
thoughts about course material.

Blog regularly
… to retain your readers.

Do I ...?

1. Do I share playlists?
   Yes ☐ No ☐

2. Do I show interest in others' music?
   Yes ☐ No ☐

3. Do I have a playlist of sounds that capture my current international experience?
   Yes ☐ No ☐

4. Do I keep up with music at home?
   Yes ☐ No ☐

29 Connect through music

... the sound of your experience

Why is this important?

We ofen remember experiences most deeply through the music we associate with them. What you listen to as a student can define your memories later. Music offers a way of connecting you to home, of crossing cultural and language boundaries, and of opening up whole new worlds of sound. The international community on campus can be an ideal chance of sharing your music and learning about what others enjoy. If you are tired of speaking in a foreign language, listening to music provides an easy way of being with friends without the need to talk. It can help with study and relaxation, too.[38]

Considering your responses

Consider whether you are making the most of what music has to offer as a means of connecting with others, capturing the ethos of your current experience for future memories and sharing with others. Create playlists to serve different purposes in your life, travel and study.

 See also Ways 14, 19, 24, 26, 28

 To do. I will ...

Music for all occasions

Make playlists

… to share, as gifts, for travel, as reminders of your experience.

Listen for study

Use classical music with a strong beat (not just your favourite music!).

For stress-busting

Play music that makes you feel good.
Dance or sing to release adrenaline and ease stress.

For cultural exchange

Share favourites from home.

Sing, or play an instrument

Improve brain function, learn something new.
Play with others. Or join a choir.

As a talking point

Listen to music popular with students or on student radio.

Listen to relaxing music

… to help you power down after a stressful day or before sleep.

To connect to home

For happy memories, or to keep up to date
with what friends are listening to back home.

30

Take your space to speak

Make your presence felt

1. Do I avoid speaking in class?

   Yes **No**

2. Do I wish I had the courage to say more?
   Yes **No**

3. Do I speak too much in class?

   Yes **No**

4. Do I lose out from not speaking?

   Yes **No**

Why is this important?

It is hard for some students to speak in class, either because this isn't the custom back home or because they lack confidence in an unfamiliar context or foreign language.[76] It also takes longer to compose thoughts in a foreign language. Such students can become 'invisible', being over-looked for social events, groupwork, trips and prizes.[77,78] On the other hand, some students take up more than their fair share of the time available. It is better for all if everyone contributes and takes the right amount of space, speaking up in class and in social life and encouraging others to contribute.

Considering your responses

If you miss out the full experience of the course or student life because you find it hard to speak or to get heard, it is worth developing strategies to take your rightful space. You deserve to be heard! Alternatively, be aware if you tend to dominate. You deserve to be heard too, but don't lose out by not getting to hear what others have to say.

 See also Ways 20, 26, 33, 36

 To do. I will …

Speak out!

Prepare in advance of class

Write out questions or comments and practise these.

Let yourself make mistakes

Don't worry too much about being perfect or you will miss chances to get heard and develop confidence.

Ask to come back to a point

If you missed the opportunity to speak, ask to return to the point and ask your question or make your point. If that isn't possible, raise it outside of class time.

Create a space to speak

If you don't have enough opportunity to consider your ideas and questions in class, form a study group or set up a discussion board or chat space to talk about things in a less pressurised context.

Contribute fairly

Don't dominate the group, and don't leave others to do all the work of speaking in class, either.

Ask the quiet students first

Give them time to collect their thoughts and encourage them to say what they can if speaking a foreign language.

31

Be sport active!

Get moving!

Why is this important?

Sports are important in most cultures and so playing them, watching them, discussing them and supporting a team can all ease social interactions. Being part of a team creates a ready group for sharing other aspects of culture. In addition, being physically active

improves health, relieves stress and even boosts academic performance.[38] If you prefer solitude, there are many ways to stay active without playing team sports, so you gain the broader benefits of physical exercise.

Considering your responses

Whether you are good, bad or indifferent at sports, you can find (or set up) a team at your level. Being a student is a great time to learn a new sport. You can join or form a team that meets mainly for fun and socialising, or one that is competitive.

See also Ways 13, 19, 26, 37

? Do I ...?

1. Do I avoid sports because I don't think I am good enough at them?

   Yes ☐ No ☐

2. Do I know a sport not usually played in this country?

   Yes ☐ No ☐

3. Is there a sport I wished I played?

   Yes ☐ No ☐

 To do. I will ...

Join the team!

Take up social exercise

Choose from the many sports and exercise clubs at your institution – a great way to gain a new social group.

Support your teams

Take an interest in the college or uni teams. Turn up to matches to cheer them on. Get to meet people, gain a new topic of conversation and feel you belong.

Stay healthy

(Or get healthy!) Ideally, use exercise that raises your heartbeat, but any is better than none.

Gain the 'feel good' factor

Physical activity triggers chemicals that make you feel happier and add to a sense of well-being.

Go to 'away' matches

Travel in the supporters' coach, and get to see more of the country whilst supporting your team!

Promote your national sport

Set up a society for your national sport. Teach it to others and experience a touch of home.

Find your sport

Sports Services can usually suggest options or create opportunities even for those who consider themselves terrible at all sport!

32

Learn the local sense of humour

Gain insights into language and culture

1. Do I know how humour differs in this country from my own?

Yes ☐ No ☐

2. Do I have good jokes to share?

Yes ☐ No ☐

3. Do I use jokes to help me understand more about how language works?

Yes ☐ No ☐

4. Do I laugh every day?

Yes ☐ No ☐

Why is this important?

Humour oils the wheels of social interactions, eases difficult situations and helps people to connect. It differs a great deal across cultures, so it is important, in an international setting, to know what would be found funny, by whom, and what might be considered to be 'odd', disrespectful or offensive. Building humour into your day has been found to reduce and prevent stress.[38] In addition, as humour usually involves a 'play' on language or expectations, then understanding a country's humour shines a light on its culture and assists your everyday language skills.

 To do. I will ...

Considering your responses

If you think humour is trivial, then think again. It can have a big effect on your social life, social network, mental health and well-being. You need a certain amount of insight into its humour to really understand a country and to exercise cultural sensitivity. You can achieve a great deal through enjoying some good comedy or sharing jokes.

 See also Ways 23, 24, 25, 41

Enjoy sharing a good joke

Learn how to tell a joke
… an excellent way to learn to use precise intonation and timing in a language – as these are usually needed for jokes to work.

Learn 'plays on language'
Find out about puns, tongue twisters and other well-known plays on language used for humour.

Watch comedy TV and video
Examine how humour is used, the different kinds of humour, and how people respond.

Find out what isn't amusing
Ask what kinds of things are not considered appropriate content for humour in the country. These might differ depending on who you are and who you ask.

Browse comedy sections
… in bookshops, to see what kind of humour sells in the country.

Buy a joke book
… to enjoy reading or to learn jokes to share with friends. See which ones make them laugh or groan.

33

Understand the academic culture

Think more like your professor

Do I ...?

1. Do I know much about the academic conventions for my course?

   Yes ☐ No ☐

2. Do these make sense to me?

   Yes ☐ No ☐

3. Do I know what this means for how marks or grades are awarded on my course?

   Yes ☐ No ☐

Why is this important?

Getting to understand academic culture and conventions is essential for both home and international students.[37] Studying at uni is different to studying at school or college, and also varies between courses and countries.[18,20] (See pages xvi–xvii.) Some differences will be obvious; others more subtle. It is important to understand exactly what is expected of you so that you can adapt your work and your approach to study accordingly. If you continue to do what you did before, it is unlikely that you will do as well on your current course.

Considering your responses

If you hadn't been aware of the importance of researching the academic culture, traditions and conventions for the country where you are studying, and for your subject and course, then find out as much as you can before your first attempt at each specific kind of assignment and at every new level of study.

To do. I will ...

 See also Ways 22, 27, 35, 38, 45

Understand 'how things are done here'

Make no assumptions

Don't expect anything to be exactly the same as back home or on previous courses: find out the differences.

اتبع التوجيهات

Check key areas

Investigate core areas of difference, outlined on pages 72–3.

请遵循这些指南

Use pre-sessional courses

Many colleges and unis run foundation or pre-sessional courses. These can be good for uncovering your assumptions about what is expected of both teachers and students.[79]

Follow rules and guidance

Read carefully the rules, regulations and guidance for the university (usually on its website) and for the course (in the course handbook or course website).

Следуйте инструкции

List and enquire

Maintain a list of everything you don't understand in the rules and regulations, and ask your tutor what these mean.

What is expected?
Key questions

Start of year
1. Do I need to be present on the course at the start of the year?
2. How will I know if I am fully registered and/or enrolled?
3. Are there any choices I have to make for this year? If so, what is the process for this?
4. Where should I go for student welcome and induction?
5. If I miss student induction, where can I access essential information that I missed?

Course documentation
1. What course documentation should I have received already? Where can I get copies?
2. Is there a course handbook (or equivalent)? If so, where can I find this?
3. Where can I see rules and regulations that apply to my course, assessment and grading?

Lectures and taught classes
1. Do I have to attend all classes?
2. What must I do if I can't attend?
3. Are students allowed to ask questions in class?
4. Am I expected to contribute during class?
5. Are classes available as a video/audio recording? If not, am I allowed to record the class?
6. Is there a schedule of topics to be covered in class that I can use to help me prepare in advance?

Groupwork
1. How much groupwork is there on my course?
2. What kinds of study are conducted through groupwork?

3. What is expected as good participation and behaviour in groupwork on this course? What is not considered good?

4. Is groupwork assessed? If so, how is it assessed? How is that weighted in my final grade?

Assessment of coursework

1. How will my work be assessed?

2. Where can I find the marking criteria?

3. Where can I find out which assessments I must submit and the submission deadlines?

4. What kinds of answers and approaches gain highest grades?

5. Are there examples of answers that I can use to understand what is expected of me?

6. What is the process for submitting work?

7. Are there penalties for late submission or other aspects of assessment?

Exams

1. Are there any exams?

2. When are these?

3. Are there class tests? If so, how do these count towards my grade?

Support for assessment

1. Is support available to help me understand requirements?

2. What kind of help is permitted, and what is not? What kind of help is considered to be 'cheating'.

3. Am I allowed help composing my answers?

4. Am I allowed help with proofreading?

Grading

1. Where can I find out about how my work is graded?

2. Am I allowed to appeal my grades? If so, what must I do and by when?

3. Is there advice available to help me make my appeal?

34 Master time management

Get time on your side!

Why is this important?
As an international student, there are so many things to see and do and absorb, so much to learn and understand, so many people to meet, and so many things to think about, that it can be hard to fit everything in. It is exciting but can also be overwhelming if not managed well. You can make best use of your time, and reduce the pressure of getting everything done, through being well-organised and using your time effectively.

Considering your responses
Consider whether your responses suggest you could benefit from better time management.[37,74] There are many different aspects to this, such as monitoring actual use of time, using time effectively, prioritising, avoiding a sense of excess time pressure, punctuality and meeting deadlines. Decide which aspects you are good at, and which could be improved.

 See also Ways 5, 16, 22, 37

? **Do I …?**

1. Do I plan ahead effectively?

  Yes ☐ **No** ☐

2. Do I keep running out of time?

  Yes ☐ **No** ☐

3. Do I have enough time to study and to fit in other things I want to do?

  Yes ☐ **No** ☐

4. Do I waste time?

  Yes ☐ **No** ☐

 To do. I will …

Beat the clock!

Prioritise!
Be realistic about how much you can really fit into a day or week. Decide what you will – and won't – do!

Know where your time goes
Monitor a whole day, week or study session occasionally to see what you really spend your time doing!

Use time saving tips
A few minutes saved here and there can add up to hours (or days!).[37]

Develop good concentration
Focus on each task in turn to reduce time lost in errors and in re-doing the work.[80]

Be systematic
Taking a logical, step-by-step approach means you are clearer about what to do. It reduces stress and helps to get it done![37,81]

Keep to schedule
Devise schedules that are realistic for you. Then stick to what you have decided.

35 Write in the right academic style

Learn the academic style of the host country

Why is this important?

Many international students are new to writing essays and reports. Even if you write these at home, you may need to write them differently elsewhere.[82,83] In the UK, essays are structured with an introduction, body and conclusion; points are organised to develop a reasoned argument, with the most important points first.[37,81] In some countries, the structure is 'thesis, antithesis, synthesis'. In others, it is a chronologically unfolding 'story'. The way you cite and discuss sources varies too. Even if it feels strange or 'wrong', use the style required for the course.

Considering your responses

If you are unsure what is expected, it is essential to find this out as early as possible. Check what is expected in terms of structure, criticality, whether or not to express personal opinion or interpretations, and how to cite sources. Don't assume it will be the same as at home. Practise writing in the style of the host country and/or your course.

 See also Ways 17, 20, 33, 38, 45

Do I ...?

1. Do I need to write essays, papers or reports for my course?

   Yes ☐ **No** ☐

2. Do I need to write essays in exams?

   Yes ☐ **No** ☐

3. Do I know the academic writing style required for my course?

   Yes ☐ **No** ☐

 Find out more

See Cottrell, S. (2019). *The Study Skills Handbook* for writing essays and reports.

 To do. I will ...

Read to support writing

Bring work from home

… or just write out an example to use instead. If you can, show tutors examples of what you are used to. It makes it easier for them to point out differences in expectations.

Read in the study language

Learn to express yourself in the specialist language of the subject. Take notice of how concepts are articulated in several textbooks and other academic sources, to help you formulate your own sentences in your work.

Read journal articles

… in the language of study, to get a sense of the academic style.

Check your understanding

… of theories, concepts and explanations. If you are not clear what you are reading, research the topic in your own language so your work is accurate.

Use the marking criteria

Make sure you know where to find these and what they mean. Check them frequently. Use them to guide the way you research and write up your assignments.

36

Build your bilingualism

Prepare to take your learning home

Do I ...?

1. Do I make a conscious effort to learn concepts in both languages?

   Yes ☐ **No** ☐

2. Do I have a system for recording information for use when I return home?

   Yes ☐ **No** ☐

3. Do I share knowledge and ideas in my home language and language of study?

   Yes ☐ **No** ☐

Why is this important?

When you return to your home country, it is likely that you will want to think about, speak about and use the knowledge gained on your course. Whilst you will want to make the most of the opportunity to learn to express yourself in the language of study, it is a good idea to develop your understanding of concepts in your home language, too. Some information, especially that involving numbers, can make more sense and be easier to remember when you grasp it in your home language.[84]

Considering your responses

If your responses suggest you are neglecting one of your languages, find ways of using both across your week. Make sure that you know how to express advanced concepts and ideas in your own language as well as in the language of study. Notice the differences in the ways that ideas are expressed in home and study languages.

 See also Ways 14, 17, 20, 50

 To do. I will ...

Say it twice!

Indicate ✔ which might be useful for you to try.

Check in own language
If you are not clear what you are reading, research the topic in your own language too. Make sure you understand the concepts.

Make bilingual notes
Split your page into a wider and narrower column. Take notes in the foreign language, using your own words. Use a tool such as Linguee[85] to help you shape your own phrases. Use the narrower column for reminders of meaning in your own language – it will save you checking again later.

Update your phrase book
When you read new words and phrases relevant to your subject, note these down alphabetically so you can find them quickly again later. Look up the equivalent in your own language. You will have this to use when you discuss the subject in your own language when you return home.

Talk about your subject in both languages
Explain complex concepts to friends (or family) whose first language is your home language – and also to native speakers of the language of the host country.

Blog in both languages
Alternate between languages in your posts – or write each post in your home language and the language of study.

37

Recharge your energy

... refresh body, mind and spirit!

Why is this important?

International student life can be exhausting. Student life, in general, can create pressure to fit in as much as you can, and that is especially so if you want to see a country and gain many new experiences. In addition, living away from home and in a different country can be more tiring. It is important to make time to rest, refresh and restore your energies. Your brain needs this in order to function well, and your body needs a rest too, in order to maintain good health and vitality.

Considering your responses

Consider whether your responses suggest that you use up a lot of mental, physical or emotional energy during the week, without sufficient time to recover your energies before doing more. If so, take care to avoid 'burn out'. This can affect academic work, and also your health. Plan varied activities for rest and relaxation each day.

 See also Ways 26, 29, 31

 Do I ...?

1. Do I race to fit in all I have to do?

   Yes ☐ No ☐

2. Do I get exhausted at times?

   Yes ☐ No ☐

3. Do I use a lot of emotional energy?

   Yes ☐ No ☐

4. Do I create time to recharge?

   Yes ☐ No ☐

To do. I will ...

Take a break!

Take five minutes!
Take plenty of short breaks when studying to restore energy and keep your mind alert.

Relax
Take a relaxing bath and curl up with a book. Or go for a walk and enjoy local nature.

Eat well
Eat nourishing food, not junk food, to maintain energy and alertness for longer.

Sleep routine
Keeping to a sleep routine helps gain sufficient good sleep to get through the day.

Rehydrate
Sip water throughout the day for energy, concentration and less stress.

Avoid 'burn out'
Take notice of your energy levels. If you get tired easily, find out why and change your routine.

Rest
Find time to pause in the day or evening, separate to sleep.

Build in variety
Changing activity can be as good as a rest. Alternate study, exercise, rest and social activities.

Maintain calm!
Being calm helps to conserve energy. Try yoga, meditation or breathing exercises.[80]

38 Understand how 'criticality' is applied

Develop critical thinking abilities

Why is this important?

Academics worldwide place a high value on making fair critical analyses of the work of experts in order to advance knowledge. Depending on the course and country, students might be expected to show respect for experts or critique published research, or demonstrate critical thinking in distinct ways.[86,87] On some courses, high grades are awarded only if work demonstrates critical reasoning, strong argument and excellent referencing. Check what is expected on your course with respect to criticality and use of expert sources.

Considering your responses

If you haven't already considered what is required in terms of critical thinking on your course, find out what is expected early on as this can make an immense difference to your grades.

1. Do I know the level of criticality expected on my course?

Yes ☐ No ☐

2. Do I know how I am expected to cite and refer to 'experts' in my work here?

Yes ☐ No ☐

3. Do I understand if, how and why this differs to what I am used to?

Yes ☐ No ☐

4. Do I know how this affects grades?

Yes ☐ No ☐

 See also
Ways 22, 33, 35, 45

 To do. I will ...

Understand how to 'critique'

Find out the expectations
Talk to your tutors, skills advisers or librarians about what kind of criticality is expected at your level of study and what exactly that means. Don't be afraid to ask for explanations and examples.

See archived examples
Ask in the library whether there are archived examples of previous students' work (with good grades) that you can read. Even if these are at a higher level, such as final year dissertations, they provide insights into how criticality is used.

Check in journal articles
Use journals produced in the country where you are studying. Check with tutors how critical analyses in these differ from what is expected at your level.

Use strong reasoning
Learn to develop a consistent argument, with conclusions based on reasons and evidence.[87]

Expressions of respect
Find out how respect for experts is conveyed on your course.

Know how to cite experts
Learn the exact methods for citing experts whose work you have used for assignments.[37,88]

39

Use the right exam preparation

... relevant to the country and level of study

 Do I ...?

1. Do I know what to expect in the exams?
   Yes ☐ No ☐
2. Do I know what kinds of exam questions are used?
   Yes ☐ No ☐
3. Do I have experience of these kinds of exam?
   Yes ☐ No ☐

Why is this important?

In some countries, exams are primarily based on memory; in others, the emphasis is on writing reasoned argument or solving problems. Some courses use a mixture of many kinds of tests, exams, presentations and practical work; others rely on just exams. To achieve good grades, you need to understand what is expected: don't assume all exams are the same as you are used to. Adapt your preparation for exams depending on what is required.[13,18]

Considering your responses

Investigate what will be required in exams. Don't be afraid to ask. Your tutors are likely to want international students to succeed but could be unaware of variations in assessment with which you are familiar. Explain what you are used to; check whether these exams will be the same. If not, ask where you can gain further guidance to prepare for them.

 To do. I will ...

 See also Ways 22, 34, 44, 46

Master exam techniques

Indicate ✔ which might be useful for you to consider or do.

Look at past papers
Ask the librarians or your tutor where you can find copies of past papers. Get familiar with the kinds of questions that are asked.

Find out what is 'good'
Look at the marking criteria for the course. Use these as a guide for exam answers too. Ask tutors what a good answer would look like for longer answers such as essays.

Practise in advance
Complete exam papers under conditions similar to your exam.[89]

Devise your own questions
Use the style of the course's exam papers. Make sure you can answer them.

Develop exam techniques
If you are not used to memory-based exams, start to learn material as you go along. Find out about techniques to help you memorise and recall information.[13,37,89]

Don't memorise the book!
Beware of memorising whole passages exactly as they are written and then reproducing these in the exam. Shape key ideas in your own words.

Feeding back the lecture?
In some countries, professors want exam answers to be based on their lectures; in others, they don't like this. Find out which approach to use.

40 Enhance your career

Boost your career opportunities

Do I ...?

1. Do I know how studying abroad could improve my career opportunities?
   Yes ☐ **No** ☐

2. Do I know how to articulate the value of my studying abroad to interest employers?
   Yes ☐ **No** ☐

3. Do I have a checklist to complete whilst abroad to enhance my career path?
   Yes ☐ **No** ☐

Why is this important?

Career enhancement is a key reason for studying abroad. For example, 75% of Chinese students said their main reason for studying abroad was for improved career prospects.[4] When choosing a uni or college, check the range of career-related services on offer, especially for international students.[90] Make full use of these on arrival. Experience of studying abroad is an asset to many careers, especially if you gain a language and develop cultural awareness. The confidence and self-reliance gained from studying abroad can also be advantageous.

Considering your responses

Employers tend to be keen to see how you made the most of the opportunities available to you whilst studying or living abroad. Consider how you would answer potential questions about your time away. If you haven't written one already, create a checklist of things to do whilst studying abroad to enhance your future career path.

 See also Ways 15, 20, 42, 47

 To do. I will …

Plan for your future

Devise a career checklist

Ask careers services for advice in compiling this to make best use of opportunities in the host country. Complete it if you can whilst there.

Understand the career path

Make sure you take courses and qualifications relevant to your ideal career role and home country.

Try out varied roles

Before settling on a career, have a go at jobs in other fields. You might find a career that suits you better.

Gain relevant experience

Know what your preferred career route really involves through a part-time or volunteering job.

Gain a career mentor

Your tutor, or uni or college career services might be able to help you find a mentor in a relevant field.

Broaden your skills

Develop a wide range of skills that will appeal to future employers.[91,92]

Take on responsibility

Demonstrate to future employers that you can be trusted with responsibility, by taking on leadership roles as a student.

Think international

Whilst abroad, investigate the opportunities for careers in the host country and those nearby.

Articulate the value

Identify what you have gained from the experience of living abroad that is of value to you and employers.

41

Learn the unspoken language

Understand the culture of communication

Why is this important?

The way we communicate non-verbally varies between cultures. What is polite or acceptable in one culture might be inconsiderate or disrespectful in others. This includes eye contact, how we greet people, say goodbye or express thanks. In some cultures, you say what you think; in others, you pick up on unspoken messages through observation and developing shared understandings.[93] Some cultures value clarity and detail; others value 'grey areas'. If you don't adapt to the communication culture, you can miss out on essential communication.[37,94]

Considering your responses

If you hadn't thought specifically about communication differences, it is useful to do so, for yourself and others on your course. Understanding differences is important to developing cross-cultural awareness. It can help you or other students to be happier and more successful on your course. When everyone is included, everyone gains.

 See also Ways 19, 24, 25, 29

 Do I ...?

1. Do I know the communication culture of the country where I am studying?

   Yes ☐ **No** ☐

2. Do I understand how my own communication norms might differ from others'?

   Yes ☐ **No** ☐

3. Do I miss opportunities because of cultural communication differences?

   Yes ☐ **No** ☐

 To do. I will ...

Don't miss out on what is being communicated

Explain the difference

Let your friends know how things are done in your country, and why, to help them understand.

Ask about the culture

Your friends, tutor or international office can help you make sense of the communication culture.

Use local forms of address

… whether formal or informal, when speaking or writing to others.

Observe the home students

Notice what they do, or don't do, in various contexts and how that differs from how you do things.

Talk to your tutor

Ask what is expected of you in class, groups, tutorials, emails, etc.

Adapt your style

As far as possible, adapt your style to the norms of the host country.

Develop self-awareness

Consider how your own communication style might be misinterpreted.

42 Build your CV and employability

Prepare for future jobs

? Do I ...?

1. Do I have a current CV/résumé?

   Yes ☐ **No** ☐

2. Do I adapt my CV to suit the job?

   Yes ☐ **No** ☐

3. Do I know what work and activities I am permitted to carry out under my visa?

   Yes ☐ **No** ☐

4. Am I actively building my CV now?

   Yes ☐ **No** ☐

Why is this important?

You will need a CV (or résumé) when looking for work whether now or in the future. If you are eligible for work whilst studying, it is a good idea to keep an up-to-date CV. Write a detailed version, then adapt it to suit the country, business and jobs for which you apply, being selective in what you include. Even if your visa prohibits work, your time as an international student offers opportunities to develop skills and qualities that increase your attractiveness to future employers. Use your time as a student wisely to build your CV.

Considering your responses

Consider whether your responses suggest there is more that you could do to build a CV/résumé relevant to jobs that interest you. If so, then identify ways that your international experience is developing you as a person and how that may be relevant to future jobs and employers. Decide on further activities to develop employability and build your CV.[92]

To do. I will ...

 See also Ways 24, 43, 47, 50

Keep developing skills and experience

Indicate ✔ which might be useful for you to do.

Keep CVs brief and clear
Let important points about your education, work, life experience, qualifications, skills and personal qualities stand out.[91]

Use the local style
Find out which style and content are typical in the host country or in whichever country you wish to work in next.

Make your CV relevant
Adapt it to the job you are applying for, so the employer feels you are interested in their business and not just in gaining *any* job.

Take on responsibility
Stand for student office or lead student projects. Let employers see you are able to take on responsible roles and are trustworthy and dependable.

Get a job (visa permitting)
Employers prefer applicants with some experience of work.

Gain new skills
Whether or not you are eligible for paid work, keep doing new things to develop skills and personal qualities relevant to your future career interests and employment.

Develop work-readiness
Develop routines and lifestyles that prepare you for work.[37,91] Get used to the application process and be ready to compete for graduate jobs.[25,26]

43

Stand for office

Make the international student voice heard!

Why is this important?

Standing for office is an excellent way of gaining from the international experience. You meet a wide range of people and learn new skills. Usually, there is training for the role, too. You tend to find out much more about how your course and institution work, which can be useful to you and your friends. By taking on responsibility, you develop your CV and gain confidence for more challenging roles in the future. In addition, being a student officer or representative, or even just standing for these roles, helps to ensure the interests of international students are taken into consideration.

Considering your responses

If your responses suggest that you hadn't thought about standing for office or don't know much about it, then it is worth finding out more about what is available at your uni or college. Don't assume you have to be a special kind of person – all kinds of students are needed in these roles in order to make sure that all students are represented.

 See also Ways 19, 30, 42, 43

 Do I ...?

1. Do I feel I could stand for office?

   Yes   **No**

2. Do I know what kinds of roles are available?

   Yes   **No**

3. Do I know how to go about gaining one of those roles?

   Yes   **No**

 Find out more

Find out how the representative systems work at your uni or college. Talk to current student reps and officers about their role, or talk to student support officers.

 To do. I will ...

Gain new skills

Be a student 'rep'
Represent the views of students on your course, or in your school, department or faculty.

Stand as student officer
… on the student union, guild, council or other democratic student bodies at your uni. Find out what roles are available, when elections are held, and when you need to submit your application to stand.

Stand for student president
Find out what the role entails. Only one person can be successful, but it could be you. Just taking part can teach you a great deal.

Be officer for a club/society
Be president, treasurer, secretary or other officer for one of the many clubs and societies on campus – or start and lead your own!

International student rep
Be a representative for the international student voice.

44 Start a discussion group

Create opportunities to discuss your perspective

Why is this important?

International students are often disadvantaged in class discussions, group work and informal conversations about study outside of class.[95] Language barriers make it harder to find the right words, at speed, to consider your own opinion and to express your thoughts. Being in an unfamiliar culture or new to class discussion can have similar effects. Other students gain experience in discussing academic issues aloud, gaining confidence in doing so. It is important to gain equivalent experience, discussing course material and shaping ideas aloud in the language of study.

Considering your responses

If you find that your course doesn't provide the class discussion that you are used to, or if you find it difficult to join in class discussions, set up a discussion group of your own. Create the right kind of informal and supportive group environment to encourage everyone to contribute.[37]

 See also Ways 14, 18, 30, 48, 50

 To do. I will ...

Shape your thinking through discussion

Ask others to form a group

Choose people who don't get to say a lot in class.

Argue your case

Find reasons to support what you think about the key issues covered on your course. Ask if others think the same way. If not, what are their reasons?

Practise using 'local style'

Notice whether there is a typical way of discussing on the course or in the country and practise that together. Notice whether it is expected that students speak at length or briefly. Is it typical to respond to others' comments? Or to be supportive or challenging? Or to ask particular kinds of questions?

Agree rules for the group

... that everyone decides and agrees together, to help the group work well and ensure everyone gets to speak.

Practise with co-nationals

To ease study on your return home, set up a group to practise in your 'home' style too.

45 Maintain academic integrity

Never submit other people's work as your own

Why is this important?

The value of a degree depends on students getting grades for work that really is their own. That means the words you use must be your own and not those of helpers, or taken from books or websites. It also means that you must cite the source of your ideas and information wherever you use these in your own work. All these should be written as a list of references, according to the method required for your course. Failure to do this correctly can mean gaining poor grades, and having to leave the uni and the country.[37,88]

Considering your responses

If you are not sure what is meant by academic integrity and plagiarism, then find out before you write and submit your work. The steps opposite make it easier to avoid plagiarism. Find out exactly what your college or uni permits in gaining help with expressing yourself if you are writing your assignments in a foreign language.

 See also Ways 22, 27, 33, 35

 Do I ...?

1. Do I know what 'plagiarism' is?
   Yes ☐ **No** ☐

2. Do I know how to cite sources in my work?
   Yes ☐ **No** ☐

3. Do I know how to avoid plagiarism?
   Yes ☐ **No** ☐

4. Do I know where to find course information about citations and plagiarism?
   Yes ☐ **No** ☐

 To do. I will ...

Avoid plagiarism

Write in your own words

If you use sentences from a book, or memorise these for exams, it will probably be treated as 'cheating'. Don't cut, paste, copy or memorise text exactly from sources.

Find out the help permitted

If people help you, then the work is not your own. Ask what kind of help is allowed for proofreading or checking that you have used language correctly.

Never submit bought essays

It is cheating. If you wish to know what essays or other assignments are like, ask your tutor.

Write the source first

Write out full details of books or articles above the notes you make when reading, so you know the source of information or ideas you refer to in your own work.

Check for copied phrases

Avoid accidental copying. Check your work carefully. If possible, use the plagiarism detection tool used for your course (such as Turnitin), or a copying detection tool such as Plagtracker.[96,97]

Follow course guidance

Find out which referencing style (e.g. Harvard, Vancouver, Chicago) your course uses for citing sources and writing references. Follow the guidance EXACTLY.

46

Join a peer mentoring scheme

... as mentor or mentee!

Why is this important?

You can gain a great deal from mentoring schemes. They can help you to settle in, meet people and make new friends. You learn more about the expectations, culture, opportunities, resources at your university and about how things work there. Mentoring schemes help international students adapt and integrate better, leading to less stress and higher pass rates.[30,31,98] Many universities provide training for mentors. Being a mentor can be valuable in future career roles and a great addition to your CV. It can increase your self-esteem and sense of belonging, whilst helping others.

Considering your responses

Peer mentors are students trained to offer basic support to other students. It is a good idea to experience being mentored (as a mentee) before becoming a mentor yourself so you understand the role from both perspectives. Find out about schemes at your university or college.

 See also Ways 12, 22, 24, 44

 Do I ...?

1. Do I know much about mentoring?
   Yes ☐ No ☐

2. Do I want to be a mentor?
   Yes ☐ No ☐

3. Would I like to have a mentor?
   Yes ☐ No ☐

4. Do I know who to contact about mentoring schemes at my university?
   Yes ☐ No ☐

 Find out more

UKCISA (2008). (In bibliography.[99])

 To do. I will ...

Gain valuable skills – and help others too!

Be a mentee
Settle in to university life with less stress and more support.

Understand the scheme
It usually involves informal support from students for a few weeks. It doesn't replace professional support nor involve proofreading or help with coursework.

Be a peer mentor
Gain confidence, skills, leadership.

Help promote the scheme
Offer to distribute leaflets or promote it on social media. Tell other students about it.

Record your learning
Keep a note of skills and understanding you gain through the process. Consider how the mentoring experience could be useful to you in other contexts, such as in future career roles.

No scheme at your uni?
Suggest that one is set up and help to get it started. Information from UKCISA may help.[99]

47

Develop leadership capacity

Step up!

Why is this important?

Being an effective leader is strongly associated with academic and career success. It also brings wider benefits such as the ability to persist through difficulties, to resist being stereotyped and to form higher aspirations for yourself in life.[100,101,102,103] Leadership involves a belief that you can lead, which is best founded on experience of leading, learning from the experience, developing leadership skills and gradually building your confidence. If you don't feel ready to lead, then this is a good time to start gaining experience, skills and confidence.

Considering your responses

If you don't think of yourself as a leader or don't know much about leadership, then it is worth considering leadership skills you might need throughout your career. There are many kinds of leader, so don't assume you couldn't be one. International students bring different perspectives to leadership, which benefits the student community as well as your own future.

 See also Ways 40, 42, 44, 46

 Do I ...?

1. Do I think of myself as a leader?

Yes ☐ No ☐

2. Do I need leadership skills to succeed in my career?

Yes ☐ No ☐

3. Do I think I could learn leadership?

Yes ☐ No ☐

4. Do I know much about leading?

Yes ☐ No ☐

 To do. I will ...

Become a rising star

Learn how to do it
Take a leadership course at your uni. If one isn't already provided, ask whether one can be set up.

Build your confidence
All leaders had their first day as a leader, where they still had much to learn. Gain understanding of the role through hands-on experience.[91]

What do you offer as leader?
How would your personal qualities and approach help you and others if you took the lead? What kind of leader would you be?

Offer to lead
Give reasons why you would be the right person to lead student or work projects, or for officer roles.

Set up your own project
You are then its leader.

Bring the international student dimension
Bring something fresh and interesting to leadership roles, drawing on your own culture.

Find a good team to help
No leader is perfect or knows everything. Consider carefully the skills, experience or characteristics in other people that would complement your own strengths.

48

Join a book club

Read for pleasure. Chat about books

Do I...?

1. Do I enjoy reading?

   Yes   No

2. Do I like talking about books?

   Yes   No

3. Do I like meeting people who enjoy reading?

   Yes   No

Why is this important?

Book clubs on campus or in a local library are a great way of developing your reading and spoken language skills and for meeting people, especially if you prefer quieter ways of socialising. They are usually free, and are easy to join or set up. Anybody can benefit, although it helps if you enjoy reading for pleasure. If you would find it easier to speak in a group where there are others who are not communicating in their first language, ask in the library or skills centre whether these could be set up at your uni or college.

 Find out more

Ask a librarian at uni. They can advise on books available in larger numbers for group use, and on how to start and promote a book club group.

Considering your responses

If your responses suggest that a book club could be for you, then have a go. Every group has its own flavour and energy, depending on who turns up. Usually, all the members decide on the next book to read, or they create a list for the term or year. You gain more from the group if you have read the book, but book clubs are usually informal and welcoming, so you can still turn up even if you haven't read or understood much of the book.

 To do. I will …

 See also Ways 14, 18, 20, 44

Link up through books

Start or join a group
It could focus on a particular genre such as sci-fi, crime, romance, international literature, etc.

Suggest things to read
Choose books that are easy to obtain through the library or are still in print to purchase.

Read the book
Enjoy it. Think about the plot, characters and use of language.

Speak in book club
Although you don't have to speak, clubs are more fun and more likely to continue if everyone joins in.

Shape your thoughts first
Have opinions about the book. If you want to feel more confident, practise saying aloud three things you liked and three you disliked about the book, and why.

Suggest a 'book swap'
Libraries often offer an event or an 'open shelf' for swapping books. You contribute a book you don't need any more, and take one contributed by someone else.

49 Share and develop food identities

Food fusion!

Do I ...?

1. Do I know what kinds of food are popular with other students?

   Yes ☐ No ☐

2. Do I know how to cook my national dish?

   Yes ☐ No ☐

3. Do I eat the same food as others?

   Yes ☐ No ☐

4. Do I share food experiences?

   Yes ☐ No ☐

Why is this important?

Everyone needs to eat, so food is a good bridge between cultures. Talking about food, trying local food, sharing food rituals and cooking together can all encourage bonding. You can share anecdotes of great (or terrible!) meals. Thinking about why people eat as they do can help you understand more about your own identity and about national and regional cultures.[104,105] Being away from home provides opportunities for experimenting with new foods, extending your palate, learning to cook, and even for inventing new meals and recognising more about your own identity.[106,107]

Considering your responses

If you are not part of the food culture at your uni, then find out more about it – it can help increase feelings of belonging and is a way of making friends. Consider ways that you and others could share local food, home cooking, national dishes and food traditions. It is useful to be able to cook a few meals that you can share with others.[36]

 To do. I will ...

 See also Ways 13, 14, 18, 19

Meet, greet and eat!

Learn a 'national dish'

Learn to cook it. Bring the recipe from home. Share it. Find out if there is a story behind the dish.

Student food identity

Students usually develop new eating habits based on what is cheap and easy to eat locally. Sharing such eating habits helps you to become part of the group.

Share in others' cultures

Enjoy being a guest in others' lives and understanding more about their food cultures and histories.

Show interest

Ask others about food back home. Most students will miss food they enjoyed and can enjoy talking about favourite meals.

Create fusion meals

Invite other students to create a meal that draws on ingredients and cooking techniques from diverse culinary traditions. Invent something new and delicious!

Organise tasting events

… of local foods or restaurants, or of each other's foods or cooking.

Worst meal, best meal?

What were your best and worst experiences so far? Which meals provide good anecdotes to share with others?

Do I ...?

1. Do I have plans in place for when the course is over?

   Yes ☐ No ☐

2. Do I keep up with events and changes in my country?

   Yes ☐ No ☐

3. Do I have a good record of my experience and contacts from study abroad?

   Yes ☐ No ☐

50 Prepare for life after the course

Ease the transition back home

Why is this important?

You have invested time, energy, emotion and money in your international study. After the big build-up to studying abroad, life after your course might seem rather vague and distant. The time to return home usually arrives faster than was imagined. Once home, after the initial excitement, it is easy to feel deflated and adrift, and to regret missed opportunities. To ease the transition, plan ahead in detail.[25,26] Ensure you do all the things on your checklist whilst abroad so you have no regrets (see pages 112–13 for 20+ list). Plan interesting things to do for when the course finishes.

Considering your responses

If you are not planning ahead for time after your course, start early. Speak to careers services and the international office about work, volunteering, travel or further study and whether these need to be organised many months in advance. Strengthen your connection to home or the next country you will be in so that moving on is enjoyable.

See also Ways 4, 5, 40, 42

To do. I will ...

Back to life as you knew it...?

Create a take-home list

... of ideas, recipes, souvenirs, music, gifts, ways of doing things.

Travel with work?

Consider voluntary schemes and summer jobs
around the world aimed at graduates.[108]

Further study?

Your uni might offer reduced fees if you graduate this course.

Get contact details

... for maintaining connections with friends and networks easily later.

Do those things!

Fit in all the things you haven't done yet! Write about it. Take photos. Make
great memories!

Keep connected

Stay well informed about home: be able to talk knowledgeably about events on
your return.

Line up a new course or job

Organise it to start after a short break once the current course ends.

Plan fun things

... to look forward to on your return.

'Welcome home'?

Arrange a party, meal or event with family and friends:
meet up with people you miss!

Habits shaper: Track your good intentions

Draw together your entries from the 'I will' boxes. Jot down the page number for easy cross reference. Select those you are keenest to do. Add a star, emoticon or **highlighting** each time you act on your intention.

I have committed to doing...	Way	Page
☺		
☺		
☺		
☺		

I have committed to doing...	Way	Page
☺		
☺		
☺		
☺		
☺		

My progress so far

Keep track of which of these 50 Ways you have started and completed (✔). If you come back to the book after a break, you can see at a glance which aspects you had intended to pursue, and decide whether to take up from where you left off.

Way	Page	Short title	Doing	Done!
1	2	Focus on the benefits		
2	4	Recognise potential challenges		
3	6	Be prepared for the unexpected		
4	8	Commit to finishing the course		
5	10	Devise a strategic plan		
6	12	Use the right psychology		
7	14	Sort out 'must do' actions early		
8	16	Organise essentials to bring with you		
9	22	Research what to buy once abroad		
10	24	Be moneywise		
11	26	Attend welcome events		
12	28	Bond with your university		
13	30	Combat homesickness		
14	32	Get socialising!		
15	34	Enjoy the cultural variety		
16	36	Make your own survival guide		
17	38	Create your own phrase book		
18	40	Connect to other international students		
19	42	Create wide social networks		
20	44	Fine-tune your language skills		
21	46	Handle classes in a foreign language		
22	48	Adapt your study skills		

List of 20+ things I want to do or gain from being an international student

List at least 20 things you want to look back on as enjoyable, satisfying or an achievement by the time you return home.

1

2

3

4

5

6

7

8

9

10

11

12

13

14

15

16

17

18

19

20

Where to find out more

About Universities

International Student
Barometer Survey (ISB)

This asks students to rate such things as the quality of welcome, support services, teaching and their overall experience. Check uni websites for their ratings.

National Rankings

Many countries have their own systems for ranking their universities. Check these for countries where you want to study.

QS University Rankings

Provides information about universities that are recognised as especially strong in each country and world region, both generally as universities and for individual subjects. www.topuniversities.com/university-rankings

University websites

Investigate courses, facilities, the area, ratings, and what other students say. Call up as many photographs as you can of the campus and area.

Choosing a course

All global areas

www.thecompleteuniversityguide.co.uk/international

In the UK, from abroad

www.ukcisa.org.uk/Information–Advice/Preparation-and-Arrival/Choosing-a-course

Complete University Guide

www.thecompleteuniversityguide.co.uk/international/International-students-the-facts/international-students-in-the-uk-real-life-experiences/

From the UK, going abroad

www.ucas.com/undergraduate/what-and-where-study/studying-overseas/applying-study-abroad

www.hotcoursesabroad.com

www.thecompleteuniversityguide.co.uk/international/

See the official sites of countries you wish to study in – usually by adding 'gov' into your search.

Financial support

study-uk.britishcouncil.org/options/scholarships-financial-support

www.gov.uk/travel-grants-students-england

www.timeshighereducation.com/student/advice/scholarships-available-us-international-students

www.internationalstudent.com/study_usa/

General information

study-uk.britishcouncil.org (A rich source of useful information on visas, travel, culture and more for those studying internationally, including for UK nationals thinking of studying overseas.)

www.ukcisa.org.uk (Advice and information for international students in the UK.)

www.studyinaustralia.gov.au/english/why-australia

www.newzealandnow.govt.nz/study-in-nz/where-what-to-study

www.usa.gov/study-in-us

Follow links from topuniversities.com for facts about countries, fees, visa requirements and application processes. You can also find out how many international students studied in the country recently.

Global data

OECD (2017). *Education at a Glance 2017. OECD Indicators* (Paris: OECD Publishing).

Project Atlas www.iie.org/en/Research-and-Insights/Project-Atlas/About-and-FAQs

Health and fitness

www.foreignstudents.com/health/nhs

www.brokeandhealthy.com/ (100 free or cheap ways to exercise.)

https://apps.beta.nhs.uk/ (A wide range of free apps from the NHS on many aspects of health.)

Language

Dictionaries

https://dictionary.cambridge.org/dictionary/

www.thefreedictionary.com/

OneLook Dictionary Search www.onelook.com

English grammar tests

www.bbc.com/bitesize/guides/zyrn9qt/test

takeielts.britishcouncil.org/prepare-test/free-practice-tests

Learning English

www.bbc.co.uk/learningenglish/english/course/tgg (The grammar gameshow.)

learnenglish.britishcouncil.org/en/
content

Dialectblog.com (A guide to different accents in the UK.)

Peevish.com (Useful for everyday speech such as colloquialism, idiom and slang.)

Managing money

Living costs

international.studentcalculator.org/
further-information/banking/login_form

Practical tips and resources

The Macmillan Student Planner (Stella Cottrell). (Updated annually.)

Advice and information

www.ucas.com/finance/managing-money

Opening a UK bank account:

Leaflet to download at bba.org.uk International Students. (British Banking Association – now part of UKfinance.org.uk)

Sharia banking in UK

www.moneyadviceservice.org.uk/en/
articles/sharia-compliant-savings

Safety abroad

www.internationalstudent.com/study-abroad/guide/safety-tips/

Stress management

Cottrell, S. (2019). *50 Ways to Manage Stress* (London: Red Globe Press).

www.mind.org.uk

Twitter

@StudentMindsOrg

#StudentMindsBlog

#mindfulstudent

Student blogs/articles

InternationalStudent.com

(International student blogs and forums.)

See pages xx–xxii.

Study skills

Cottrell, S. (2019). *The Study Skills Handbook*, 5th edn (London: Red Globe Press).

Cottrell, S. (2012). *The Exam Skills Handbook: Achieving Peak Performance*, 2nd edn (London: Red Globe Press).

Cottrell, S. (2019). *50 Ways to Boost Your Grades* (London: Red Globe Press).

Cottrell, S. (2014). *Dissertations and Project Reports: A Step by Step Guide* (London: Red Globe Press).

Support as a student

study-uk.britishcouncil.org/planning/advice-support

The Macmillan Student Planner (Stella Cottrell). (Provides details of organisations that offer specialist support for international and other students in the UK, updated annually.)

Travel

StudentUniverse and STA Travel (Specialise in student bookings.)

Skyscanner, Travel Supermarket, or Momondo – for price comparisons.

www.sleepinginairports.net/ The Guide to Sleeping in Airports

Time management and planning

Cottrell, S. *The Macmillan Student Planner* (London: Red Globe Press). (For organising all aspects of life as a student and planning your time.)

Cottrell, S. (2019). *50 Ways to Manage Time Effectively* (London: Red Globe Press).

Visas

www.ukcisa.org.uk (UK)

www.internationalstudent.com/study_usa/preparation/student-visa/ (USA)

For other countries, see the embassy website for the country where you intend to study.

Working abroad

https://globalgraduates.com/work-abroad

www.indeed.co.uk/International-Graduate-jobs

www.prospects.ac.uk/jobs-and-work-experience/working-abroad

https://targetjobs.co.uk/careers-advice/working-abroad

https://targetjobs.co.uk/careers-advice/international-students

www.studentuniverse.co.uk/work-abroad

Writing blogs

How to start a blog
www.theblogstarter.com
www.bloggingbasics101.com

Free hosting platforms for blogs
These sites host basic blogs for free
but charge for more complex sites:
www.wix.com
www.weebly.com
https://wordpress.com/
www.blogger.com

Get more advice from:
www.hostingadvice.com

References and bibliography

References
1. Bohm, A., Davis, D., Meares, D. and Pearce, D. (2002). *Global student mobility 2025: Forecasts of the global demand for international education* (Canberra, Australia: IDP Education). Available at: www.foresightfordevelopment.org/sobipro/54/333-global-student-mobility-2025-forecasts-of-the-global-demand-for-international-higher-education [Accessed 11 March 2019].
2. ICEF Monitor (2014). *The state of international student mobility in 2015.* [online] Accessed at http://monitor.icef.com/2015/11/the-state-of-international-student-mobility-in-2015/ [Accessed 31 August 2018].
3. OECD (2017). *Indicator C4. Education at a Glance 2017*. OECD Indicators. (Paris: OECD Publishing). [online] Available at: www.oecdilibrary.org/education/education-at-a-glance_19991487 [Accessed 31 August 2018].
4. Institute of International Education (2015). *What International students think about U.S. higher education: attitudes and perceptions of prospective students from around the world.* [online] Available at: www.iie.org/Research-and-Insights/Publications/What-International-Students-Think-About-US-Higher-Education [Accessed 31 August 2018], pp.10–11.
5. Zong, J. and Batlova, J. (2018). *International Students in the United States.* [online] Available at: www.migrationpolicy.org/article/international-students-united-states [Accessed 31 August 2018].
6. UUK (2017). *International Facts and Figures.* [online] Available at: www.universitiesuk.ac.uk/policy-and-analysis/reports/Pages/international-facts-figures-2017.aspx [Accessed 11 March 2019].
7. Araiza, M. J. and Kutugata, A. (2013). 'Understanding stress in international students of higher education in a Mexican private university'. *Procedia – Social and Behavioral Sciences*, 106, pp. 3184–94.
8. Balin, E., Anderson, N. M., Chudasama, S. Y., Kanagasingam, S. K. and Zhang, L. (2016). 'Working with International Students in the U.S. and Beyond: A Summary of Survey Research by NCDA International Student Services Committee'. *Journal of International Students*, 6(4), pp. 1053–61.
9. Hwang, E., Martirosyan, N. M. and Moore, G. W. (2016). 'A review of literature on adjustment issues of international students: Recommendations for future practices and research', in K. Bista and C. Foster (eds.) *Global perspectives and local challenges surrounding international student mobility* (Hearsay, PA: IGI Global).
10. Wang, C., Li, X., O'Kane, J., Mao, Z. and Zhang, W. (2015). 'An exploration of the readiness, challenges, and expected support for their overseas study of Chinese business and management programme students'. *Higher Education Quarterly*, 69(4), pp. 314–41.
11. Belford, N. (2017). 'International Students from Melbourne Describing Their Cross-Cultural Transitions Experiences: Culture Shock, Social Interaction, and Friendship Development'. *Journal of International Students*, 7(3), pp. 499–521.

12. Bargiela, D. V. (2017). 'First weeks of Uni life'. *ISEJ*, Volume 5(1) Spring/Summer.
13. Karaman, D. (2017). 'My study abroad experience in Perth, Australia'. *ISEJ – International Student Experience Journal*, 5(1).
14. World Education News and Reviews, wenr.wes.org
15. Lee, B., Farruggia, S. P. and Brown, G. T. L. (2013). 'Academic difficulties encountered by East Asian international students in New Zealand'. *Higher Education Research & Development*, 32(6), pp. 915–31.
16. Neves, J. and Hillman, N. (2017). *Student Academic Experience Survey* (Hepi and HEA), [online] Available at: www.hepi.ac.uk/wp-content/uploads/2017/06/2017-Student-Academic-Experience-Survey-Final-Report.pdf [Accessed 31 August 2018].
17. Ramos, A. (2014). 'The Chinese International Student Experience in a Time of Increased Enrolment at the University of California, Santa Barbara'. *International Student Experience Journal*, 2(2), pp. 2–6.
18. Fowdy, T. (2016). *Making the most out of your Hong Kong Experience*. [online] Available at: www.thechairmansbao.com/making-hong-kong-exchange-experience/ [Accessed 3 September 2018].
19. Aljuwaiber, A. (2016). 'Studying MBA Abroad: Integrating Theory with Practice'. *International Student Experience Journal*, 4(1) Spring/Summer, Isejournal.weebly.com
20. Mulumbi, M. (2018). *International perspective: a Zambian student in Australia*. [online] Available at: www.timeshighereducation.com/student/blogs/international-perspective-zambian-student-australia [Accessed 31 August 2018].
21. Seviour, M. (2016). 'From Japan to the UK: The academic journeys of two fashion design students'. *International Student Experience Journal*, 4(2).
22. Shiau, H-C. (2017). 'Photograph sharing on social media and intercultural friendships in the US: A perspective from Taiwanese exchange students'. *International Student Experience Journal*, 5(1).
23. Aderotoye, O. (2017). *Studying in Ghana: The Best Decision I've Ever Made*. [online] Available at: www.isepstudyabroad.org/articles/474 [Accessed 3 September 2018].
24. Ludkovsky, A. and Ali, Z. J. (2017). 'Cultural Project'. *International Student Experience Journal*, 5 (1).
25. Matsumoto, R. (2018). *A year in London: figuring out this whole job hunting thing*. [online] Available at: www.timeshighereducation.com/student/blogs/year-london-figuring-out-whole-job-hunting-thing [Accessed 3 September 2018].
26. Matsumoto, R. (2018). *A year in London: a bittersweet departure*. [online] Available at: www.timeshighereducation.com/student/blogs/year-london-bittersweet-departure [Accessed 3 September 2018].
27. Nolan, M. (2016). 'From the U.S. to the UK: My Exchange Experience'. Student Article, *International Student Experience Journal*, 4(1).
28. Ryabchina, V. (2016). 'Welcome to the Bubble'. *International Student Experience Journal*, 4(1).
29. Shkvorchenko, S. (2017). 'A foundation for writing your first academic essay'. *International Student Experience Journal*, 5(1) Spring/Summer.
30. Graham, S. C. (2018). 'Small Group Mentoring of International Undergraduate Students: A Pilot Program'. *International Student Experience Journal*, 5(2).

31. Ragavan, S. K. (2014). 'Peer mentoring for international students in a UK law school: lessons from a pilot case study'. *Innovations in Education & Teaching International*, 51(3), pp. 292–302.

32. Ang, P. L. D. and Liamputtong, P. (2008). '"Out of the Circle": International students and the use of university counselling services'. *Journal of Research in International Education*, 5, pp.131–54.

33. Khawaja, N. G. and Dempsey, J. (2007). 'Psychological distress in international university students: An Australian study'. *Australian Journal of Guidance and Counselling*, 17, pp. 13–27.

34. Khawaja, N. G. and Dempsey, J. (2008). 'A comparison of international and domestic tertiary students in Australia'. *Australian Journal of Guidance and Counselling*, 18, pp. 30–46.

35. Schulmann, P. and Choudaha, R. (2014). 'International retention and success: A comparative perspective'. *World Education News and Reviews*, 5 September 2015.

36. Cottrell, S. (updated annually). *The Macmillan Student Planner* (London: Red Globe Press).

37. Cottrell, S. (2019). *The Study Skills Handbook* (5th edn) (London: Red Globe Press).

38. Cottrell, S. (2019). *50 Ways to Manage Stress* (London: Red Globe Press).

39. bba.org.uk/publication/leaflets/international-students/ [Accessed 3 September 2018]. (British Banking Association – now part of UKfinance.org.uk) Leaflet on opening bank account.

40. Smith, R. and Khawaja, N. (2011). 'A review of the acculturation experiences of international students'. *International Journal of Intercultural Relations*, 35(6), pp. 699–713.

41. Lee, J.-S., Koeske, G. F. and Sales, E. (2004). 'Social support buffering of acculturative stress: A study of mental health symptoms among Korean international students'. *International Journal of Intercultural Relations*, 28, pp. 399–414.

42. Glass, C. R. and Westmont, C. M. (2014). 'Comparative effects of belongingness on the academic success and cross-cultural interactions of domestic and international students'. *International Journal of Intercultural Relations*, 38, January 2015, pp. 106–19.

43. Toyokawa, T. and Toyokawa, N. (2002). 'Extracurricular activities and adjustment of Asian international students: A study of Japanese students'. *International Journal of Intercultural Relations*, 26(4), pp. 363–79.

44. Swami, V., Arteche, A., Chamorro-Premuzic, T. and Furnham, A. (2010). 'Sociocultural Adjustment among Sojourning Malaysian Students in Britain: A Replication and Path Analytic Extension'. *Social Psychiatry Psychiatric Epidemiology,* 45(1), pp. 57–65.

45. Sawir, E., Marginson, S., Deumert, A., Nyland, C. and Ramia, G. (2007). 'Loneliness and International students: An Australian study'. *Journal of Studies in International Education*, 12, pp. 148–80.

46. Kelly, P. and Moogan, Y. (2012). 'Culture shock and higher education performance: Implications for teaching'. *Higher Education Quarterly*, 66(1), pp. 24–46.

47. Biasi, V., Mallia, L., Russo, P. et al. (2018). 'Homesickness experience, distress and sleep quality of first-year university students dealing with academic environment'. *Journal of Educational Research*, 8(1), pp. 9–17.

48. Poyrazli, S. and Lopez, M. D. (2007). 'An exploratory study of perceived discrimination and homesickness: A comparison of international students and American students'. *The Journal of Psychology*, 141, pp. 263–80.

49. Thurber, C.A. and Walton, E. A. (2012). 'Homesickness and adjustment in university students'. *Journal of American College Health*, 60(5), 415–19.
50. Lemoana, B. (2018). *South African studying in the Netherlands*. [online] Available at: www.timeshighereducation.com/student/blogs/international-perspective-south-african-studying-netherlands [Accessed 31 August 2018].
51. Yadav, S. (2018). *International perspective: an Indian student in Spain*. [online] Available at: www.timeshighereducation.com/student/blogs/international-perspective-indian-student-spain
52. United Nations Educational, Scientific and Cultural Organization (UNESCO) (2013). *Intercultural Competences: Conceptual and Operational Framework* (Paris, France: UNESCO).
53. Allhouse, M. (2017). 'Creating a Student Union social learning space for international students'. *International Student Experience Journal*, 5(1) Spring/Summer, Isejournal. weebly.com
54. Wei, M., Ku, T-K. and Liao, Y-H. K. (2011). 'Minority stress and college persistence attitudes among African American, Asian American, and Latino students: Perception of university environment as a mediator'. *Cultural Diversity and Ethnic Minority Psychology. American Psychological Association*, 17(2), pp. 195–203.
55. Wei, M., Liao, Y-H, K., Heppner, P., Chao, C-L. R. and Ku, T-K. (2012). 'Forbearance coping, identification with heritage culture, acculturative stress, and psychological distress among Chinese international students'. *Journal of Counseling Psychology American Psychological Association*, 59(1), pp. 97–106.
56. Rienties, B. and Nolan, E-M. (2014). 'Understanding friendship and learning networks of international and host students using longitudinal social network analysis'. *International Journal of Intercultural Relations*, 41, pp. 165–80.
57. Kashima, E. S. and Loh, E. (2006). 'International students' acculturation: Effects of international, conational, and local ties and need for closure'. *International Journal of Intercultural Relations*, 30, pp. 471–85.
58. Tseng, W-C. and Newton, F. B. (2002). 'International students' strategies for wellbeing'. *College Student Journal*, 36(4), p. 591.
59. Ying, Y. and Han, M. (2006). 'The contribution of personality, acculturative stressors, and social affiliation to adjustment: A longitudinal study of Taiwanese international students in the United States'. *International Journal of Intercultural Relations*, 30(5), pp. 623–35.
60. Li, A. and Gasser, M. B. (2005). 'Predicting Asian international students' sociocultural adjustment: A test of two mediation models'. *International Journal of Intercultural Relations*, 29(5), pp. 571–6.
61. Hechanova-Alampay, R., Beehr, T. A., Christiansen, N. D. and Van Horn, R. K. (2002). 'Adjustment and strain among domestic and international student sojourners: A longitudinal study'. *School Psychology International*, 23(4), pp. 458–74.
62. Rasmi, S., Safdar, S. and Lewis, J. R. (2009). 'A longitudinal examination of the MIDA Model with international students (42-57)', in A. Chybicka, S. Safdar and A. Kwiatkowska (eds.) *Culture and Gender: An Intimate Relation* (Gdanskie Wydawnictwo Psychologiczne: Gdansk, Poland).

63. Zhang, J. and Goodson, P. (2011). 'Predictors of international students' psychosocial adjustment to life in the United States: a systematic review'. *International Journal of Intercultural Relations*, 35, pp. 139–62.

64. The International Student Barometer. [online] Available at: www.igraduate.org/services/international-student-barometer/ [Accessed 31 August 2018].

65. Zhang, Z. and Brunton, M. (2007). 'Differences in living and learning: Chinese international students in New Zealand'. *Journal of Studies in International Education*, 11, pp. 124–40.

66. See www.ef.co.uk/english-resources/english-idioms/ [Accessed 31 August 2018].

67. See https://americanliterature.com/english-language-idioms

68. YouthSight (2013). *Psychological distress in the UK student population: Prevalence, timing and accessing support. Final research findings.* [online] Available at: www.nightline.ac.uk/wp-content/uploads/2014/08/Psychological-distress-prevalence-timings-accessing-support-Aug-2014.pdf [Accessed 11 March 2019].

69. Hanassab, S. (2006). 'Diversity, international students, and perceived discrimination: Implications for educators and counselors'. *Journal of Studies in International Education*, 10, pp. 157–72.

70. Liao, K. Y-H., Wei, M., Ku, T.-Y., Russell, D. W. and Mallinckrodt, B. (2008). 'Moderating effects of three coping strategies and self-esteem on perceived discrimination and depressive symptoms: A minority stress model for Asian international students'. *Journal of Counseling Psychology*, 55, pp. 451–62.

71. Dao, T. K., Lee, D. and Chang, H. L. (2007). 'Acculturation level, perceived English fluency, perceived social support level, and depression among Taiwanese international students'. *College Student Journal*, 41, pp. 287–95.

72. Yeh, C. J. and Inose, M. (2003). 'International students' reported English fluency, social support satisfaction, and social connectedness as predictors of acculturative stress'. *Counselling Psychology Quarterly*, 2003, pp. 15–28.

73. NHS [online] Available at: www.nhs.uk.

74. Cottrell, S. (2019). *50 Ways to Manage Time Effectively* (London: Red Globe Press).

75. Lin, H. T. and Yuan, S.M. (2006). 'Taking blog as a platform of learning reflective journal'. *ICWL*, 2006, pp. 38–47.

76. MacIntyre, P. D. (2007). 'Willingness to communicate in the second language: Understanding the decision to speak as a volitional process'. *Modern Language Journal*, 91(4), pp. 564–76.

77. Newsome, L. K. and Cooper, P. (2016). 'International students' cultural and social experiences in a British university: "Such a hard life [it] is here"'. *Journal of International Students*, 6(1), pp. 195–215.

78. Wei, M., Heppner, P. P., Mallen, M. J., Ku, T.-Y., Liao, K. Y-H. and Wu, T-F. (2007). 'Acculturative stress, perfectionism, years in the United States, and depression among Chinese international students'. *Journal of Counseling Psychology*, 54, pp. 385–94.

79. Elmslie, R. and Lewis, S. (2016). 'Student identity: Transition through project work'. *International Student Experience Journal*, 4(2).

80. Cottrell, S. (2018). *Mindfulness for Students* (London: Red Globe Press).

81. Cottrell, S. (2014). *Dissertations and Project Reports. A Step by Step Guide* (London: Red Globe Press).

82. Saravanamuthu, K. and Yap, C. (2014). 'Pedagogy to empower Chinese Learners to adapt to western learning circumstances: a longitudinal case-study'. *Cambridge Journal of Education*, 44(3), pp. 361–84.

83. Khozaei, F., Naidu, S., Khozaei, Z. and Salleh, N. A. (2015). 'An exploratory study of factors that affect the research progress of international PhD students from the Middle East'. *Education and Training*, 57(4), pp. 448–60.

84. Swain, M. (2013). 'The inseparability of cognition and emotion in second language learning'. *Language Teaching*, 46(2), pp. 195–207.

85. Linguee [online] Available at: www.linguee.com

86. Alnajjar, M. and Altamimi, S. (2016). 'Autonomy and critical thinking as threshold concepts in Higher Education'. *ISEJ*, 4(2) Autumn/Winter, [online] Available at: Isejournal.weebly.com [Accessed 3 September 2018].

87. Cottrell, S. (2017). *Critical Thinking Skills* (3rd edn) (London: Red Globe Press).

88. Pears, R. and Shields, G. (2019). *Cite Them Right: The Essential Referencing Guide* (11th edn) (London: Red Globe Press).

89. Cottrell, S. (2012). *The Exam Skills Handbook: Achieving Peak Performance* (2nd edn) (London: Red Globe Press).

90. Crockett, S. A. and Hays, D. G. (2011). 'Understanding and responding to the career counseling needs of international college students on US campuses'. *Journal of College Counseling*, 14(1), pp. 65–79.

91. Cottrell, S. (2015). *Skills for Success: Personal Development and Employability* (3rd edn) (London: Red Globe Press).

92. Cottrell, S. (2019). *50 Ways to Boost Your Employability* (London: Red Globe Press).

93. Scudamore, R. (2013). *Engaging home and international students: A guide for new lecturers*. [online] Available at: www.heacademy.ac.uk/system/files/ rachelscudamorereportfeb2013.pdf [Accessed 11 March 2019].

94. British Council. *The value of intercultural fluency*. [online] Available at: www.britishcouncil. org/education/skills-employability/intercultural-fluency/value-benefits [Accessed 21 July 2018].

95. Safipour, J., Wenneberg, S. and Hadziabdic, E. (2017). 'Experience of education in the international classroom: A systematic literature review'. *Journal of International Students*, 7(3), pp. 806–24.

96. Turnitin. [online] Available at: www.turnitin.com [Accessed 31 August 2018].

97. Plagtracker. [online] Available at: www.plagtracker.com [Accessed 31 August 2018].

98. Thomson, C. and Esses, V. M. (2016). 'Helping the transition: Mentorship to support international students in Canada'. *Journal of International Students*. 6(4), pp. 873–86.

99. UKCISA (2008). *Mentoring schemes for international students: A practical guide*. [online] Englishuk.com UKCISA, www.ukcisa.org.uk/Research–Policy/Resource-bank/ resources/17/Mentoring-schemes-for-international-students-a-practical-guide [Accessed 2 September 2018].

100. Day, D. V., Harrison, M. M. and Halpin, S. M. (2009). *An Integrative Approach to Leader Development* (New York: Routledge).

101. Hannah, S. T., Avolio, B. J., Luthans, F. and Harms, P. D. (2008). 'Leadership efficacy: Review and future directions'. *Leadership Quarterly*, 19(6), pp. 669–92.

102. Machida, M. and Schaubroeck, J. (2011). 'The role of self-efficacy beliefs in leadership development'. *Journal of Leadership & Organizational Studies*, 18(4), pp. 459–68.
103. Ngyuen, D. H. K. (2016). 'Student success through leadership self-efficacy: A comparison of international and domestic students'. *Journal of International Students*, 6(4), pp. 829–42.
104. Ciliotta-Rubery, A. (2016). 'Food identity and its impact upon the study abroad experience'. *Journal of International Students*, 6(4), pp. 1062–8.
105. Montanari, M. (2006). *Food is Culture* (New York: Columbia University Press).
106. Andrade, M. (2006). 'International student perspective: Integration or cultural integrity?'. *Journal of College Student Retention*, 8(1), pp. 57–81.
107. Counihan, C. and Van Esterik, P. (2013). *Food and Culture: A Reader* (New York, NY: Routledge).
108. VSO. Available at: www.vsointernational.org [Accessed 3 September 2018].

Bibliography

1. Bartram, B. (2007). 'The sociocultural needs of international students in higher education: A comparison of staff and student views'. *Journal of Studies in International Education*, 11(2), pp. 205–14.
2. Lee, J. J. and Rice, C. (2007). 'Welcome to America? International student perceptions of discrimination'. *Higher Education*, 53, 381–409.
3. Project Atlas. [online] Available at: www.iie.org/en/Research-and-Insights/Project-Atlas/About-and-FAQs [Accessed 31 August 2018].
4. Tang, X., Collier, D. A. and Witt, A. (2018). 'Qualitative Study on Chinese Students' Perception of U.S. University Life'. *Journal of International Students*. [online] 8(1), pp. 151–178 ISSN: 2162–3104.
5. Yi, J. K., Lin, J.-C. G. and Kishimoto, Y. (2003). 'Utilization of counseling services by international students'. *Journal of Instructional Psychology*, 30, pp. 333–42.

Index

Notes